EASY PIANO SHEET MUSIC

SONGBOOK FOR KIDS

Beginners First Book with
Easy to Play Popular,
Classic and Christmas
Songs

Part 2

TABLE OF CONTENTS

Are You Sleeping? 4

Baa, Baa, Black Sheep 5

Bingo 6

Five Little Ducks 8

Greensleeves 10

Heads and Shoulders Knees and Toes 12

Hickory Dickory Dock 14

Humpty Dumpty 15

I Gave My Love a Cherry (The Riddle Song) 16

Joy to the World 18

London Bridge Is Falling Down 19

Mozart Quaternário-2 (8/8) 20

One Little Finger 21

Oh My Darling, Clementine 22

Oh! Dem Golden Slippers 24

Oh! You Beautiful Doll 26

Pop! Goes the Weasel 28

Rain, Rain, Go Away 29

Ring Around the Rosie 30

Row, Row, Row Your Boat 32

The Mulberry Bush 33

Shoo Fly, Don't Bother Me 34

Silent Night 36

Sing a Song of Sixpence 38

Take Me Out to the Ball Game 40

The Ants Go Marching 42

The Farmer in the Dell 44

The More We Get Together 46

The Red River Valley 48

This Little Light of Mine 49

The Yellow Rose of Texas 50

Three Blind Mice 52

Twinkle Twinkle Little Star 53

We Wish You a Merry Christmas 54

White Christmas 56

Danny Boy 58

You Are My Sunshine 61

I've Been Working on the Railroad 62

Old King Cole 65

Polly Wolly Doodle 68

GET YOUR FREE BONUS PIANO BOOK! 71

Are You Sleeping?

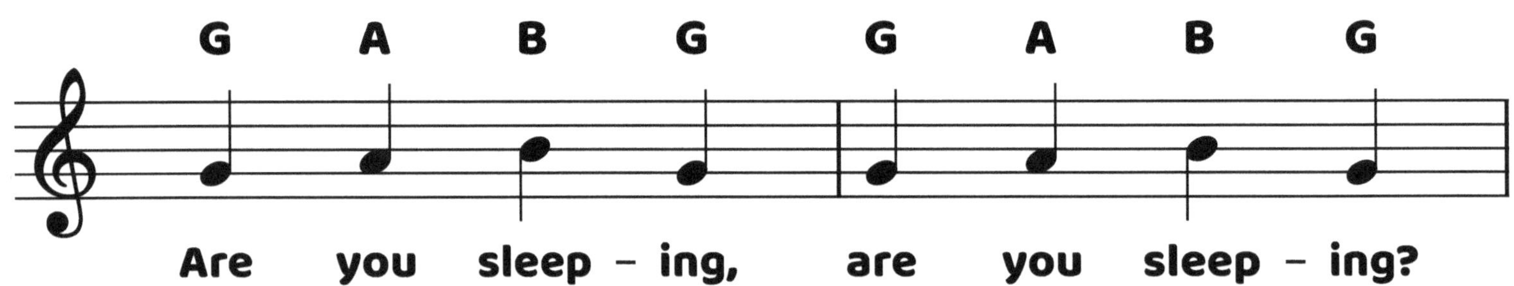

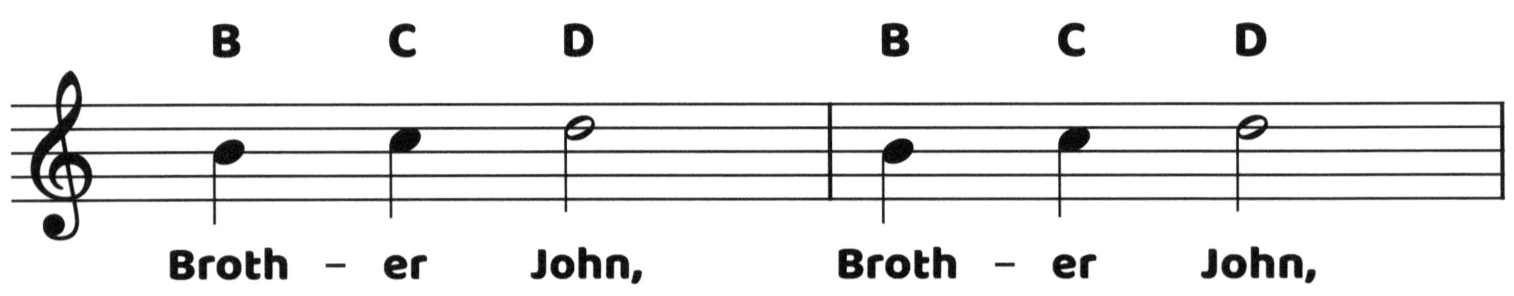

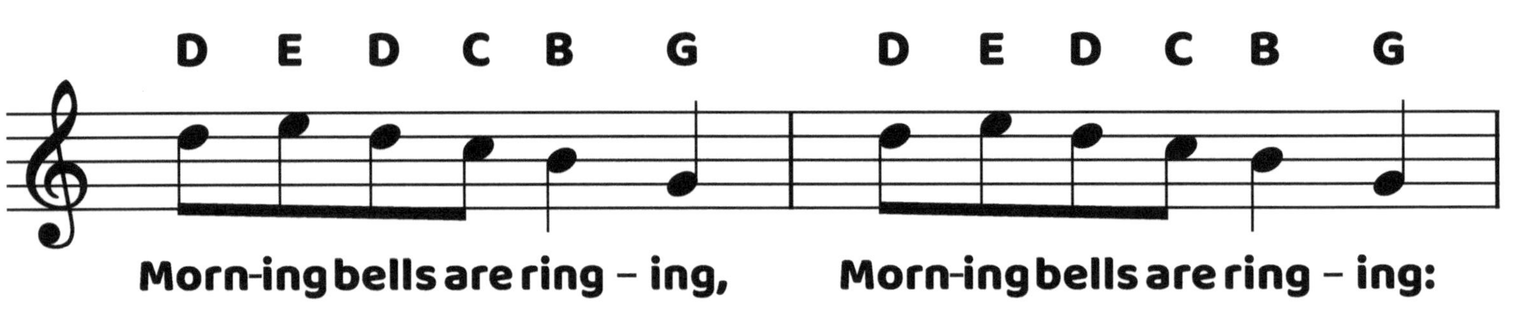

Baa, Baa, Black Sheep

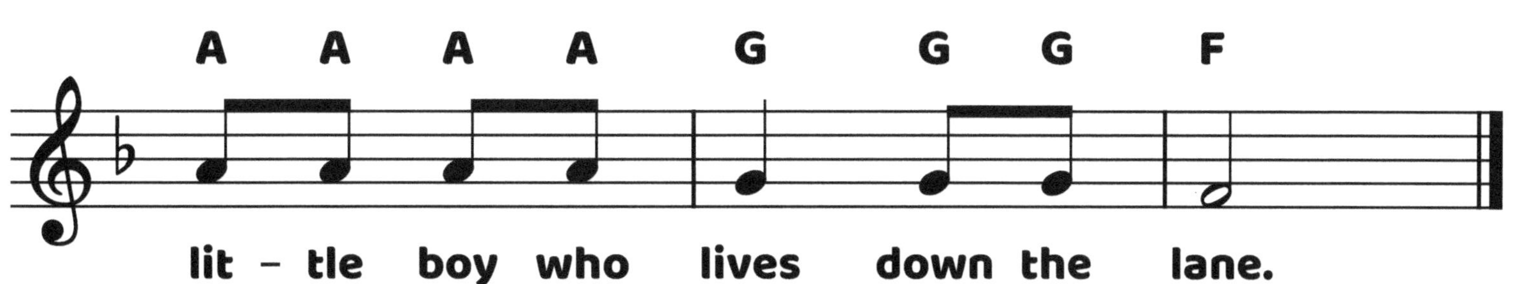

Bingo

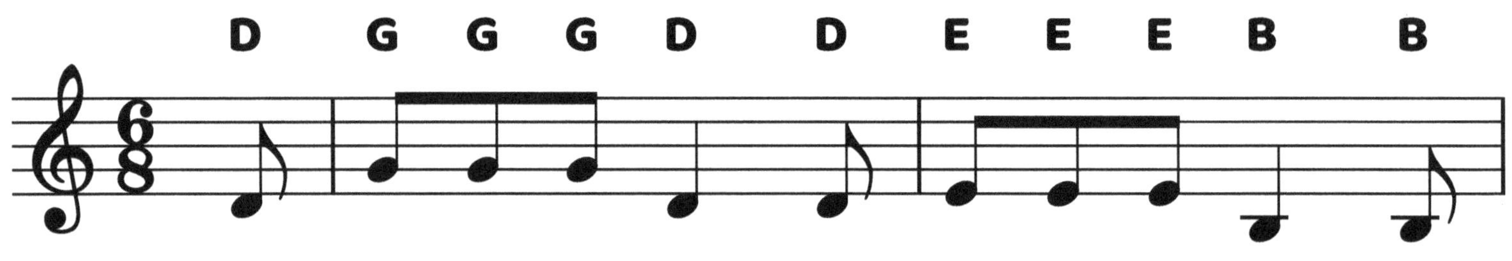

D   G   G   G   D   D   E   E   E   B   B
There was an old dog lay at the mill door and

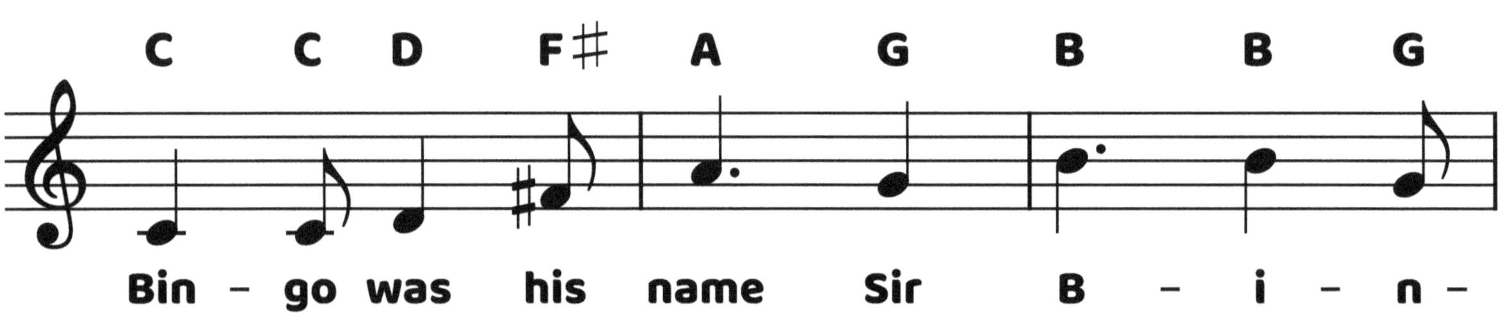

C   C   D   F#   A   G   B   B   G
Bin - go was his name Sir B - i - n -

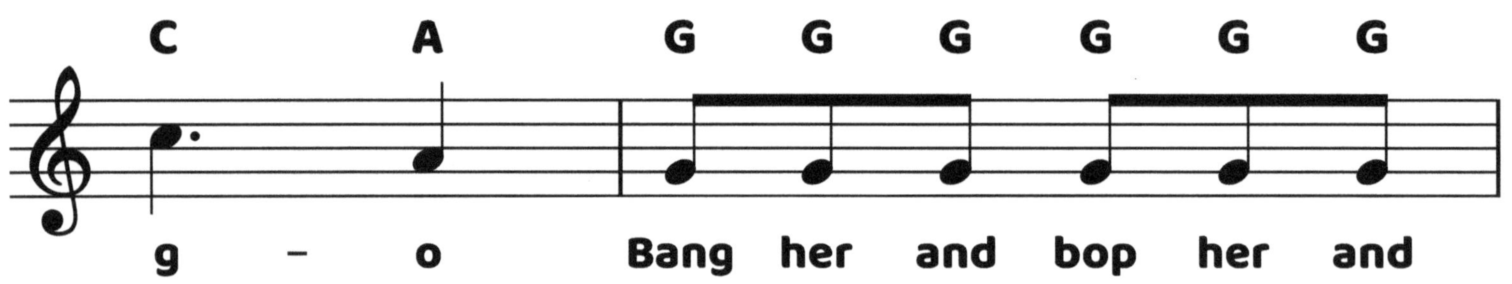

C   A   G   G   G   G   G   G
g - o Bang her and bop her and

G   G   G   G   G   G   C   C   A   D
kick her and cop her and Bin - go was his

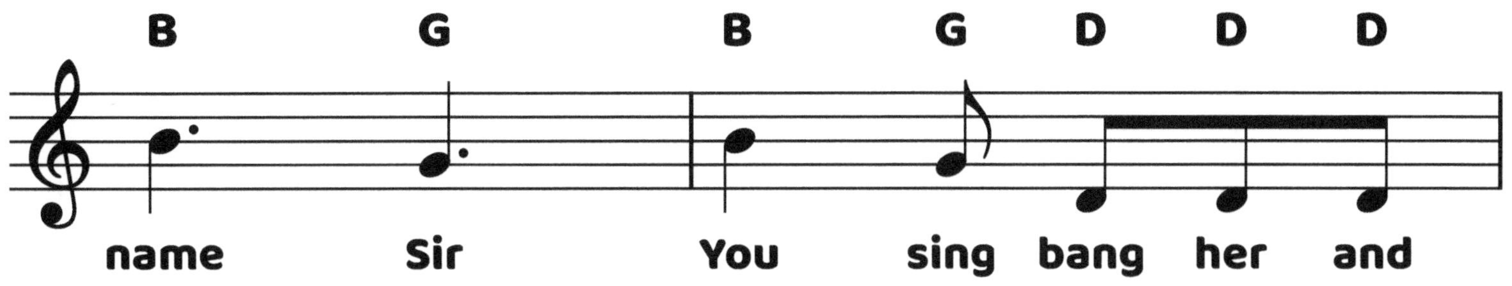

B G B G D D D
name Sir You sing bang her and

C A F# F# D B G D D D
I sing bop her and you sing kick her and

C A F# F# D G G G G G G
I sing cop her And Bang her and bop her and

G G G G G G C C A D B G
kick her and cop her and Bin – go was his name Sir

Five Little Ducks

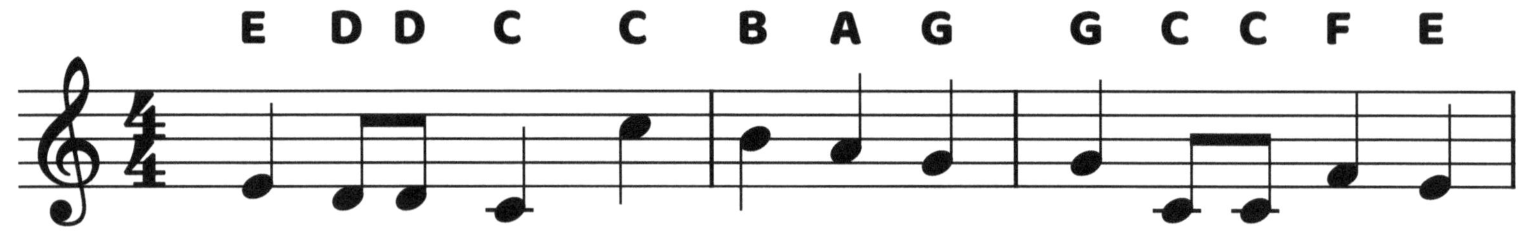

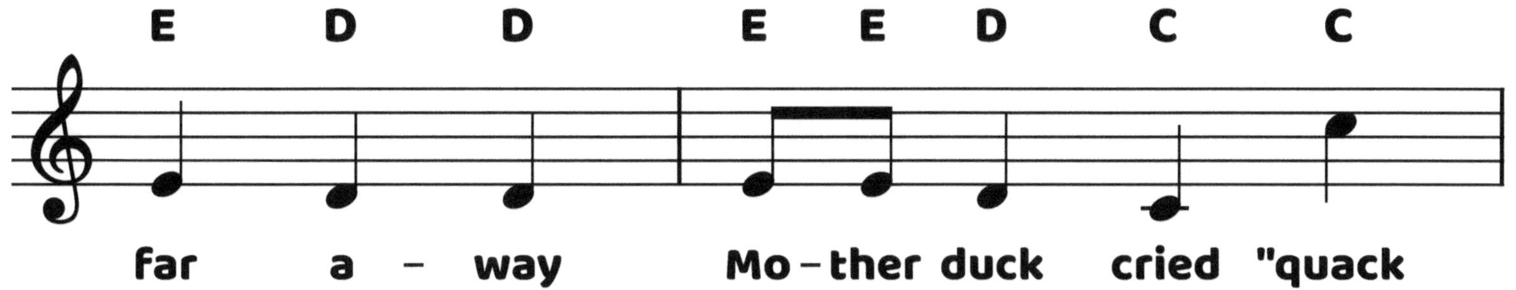

E D D   E E D C C
far a - way   Mo-ther duck cried "quack

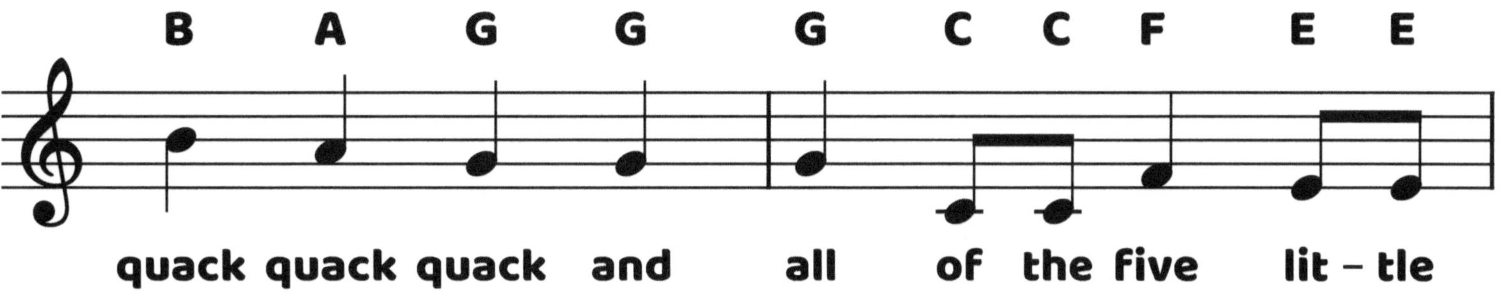

B A G G   G C C F E E
quack quack quack and   all of the five lit-tle

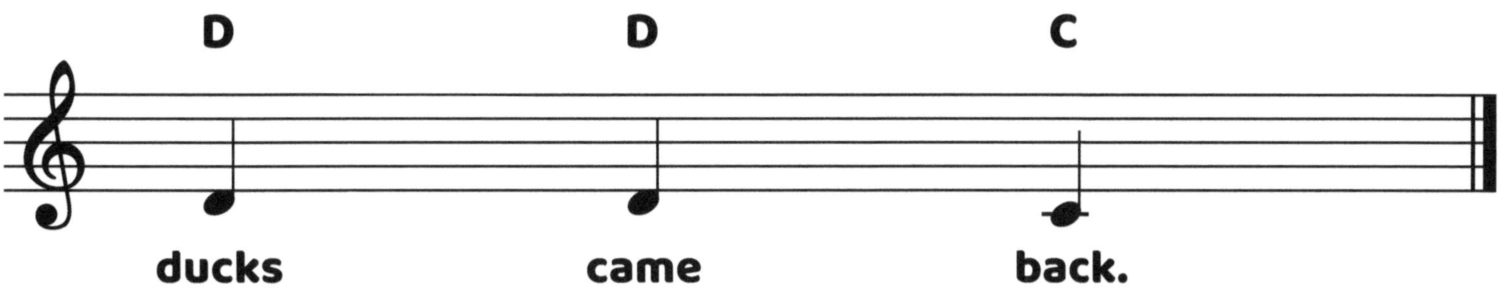

D   D   C
ducks   came   back.

Greensleeves

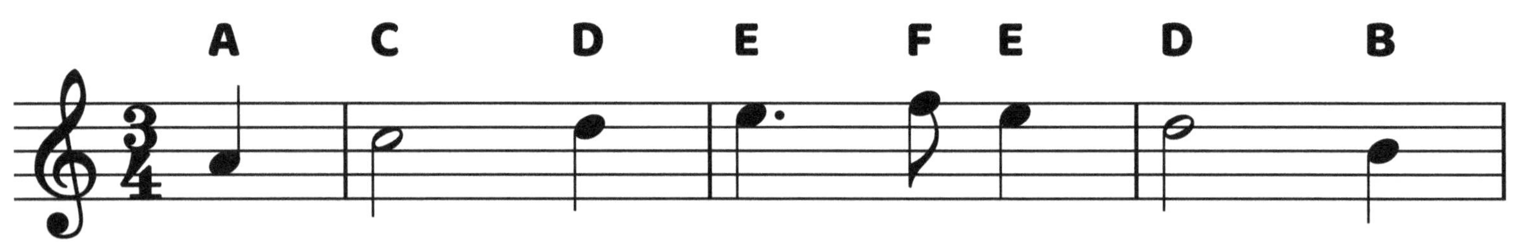

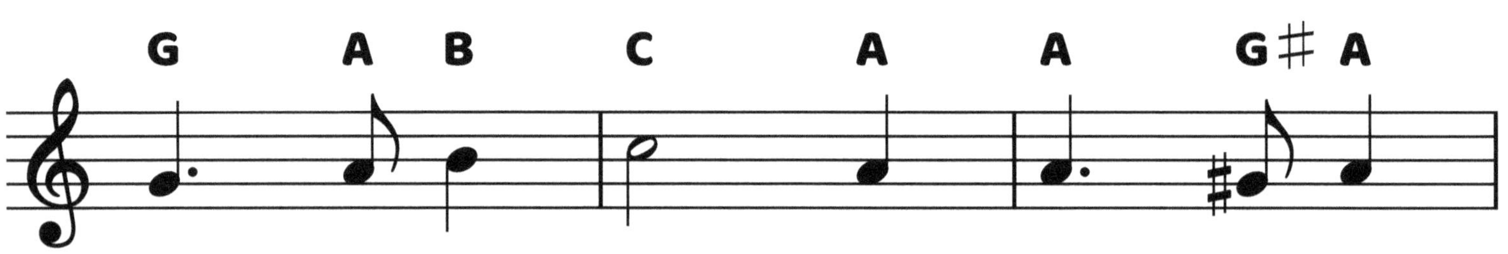

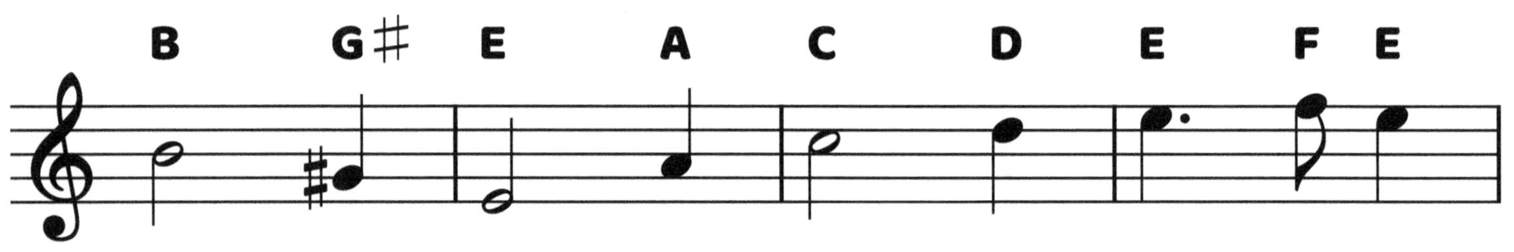

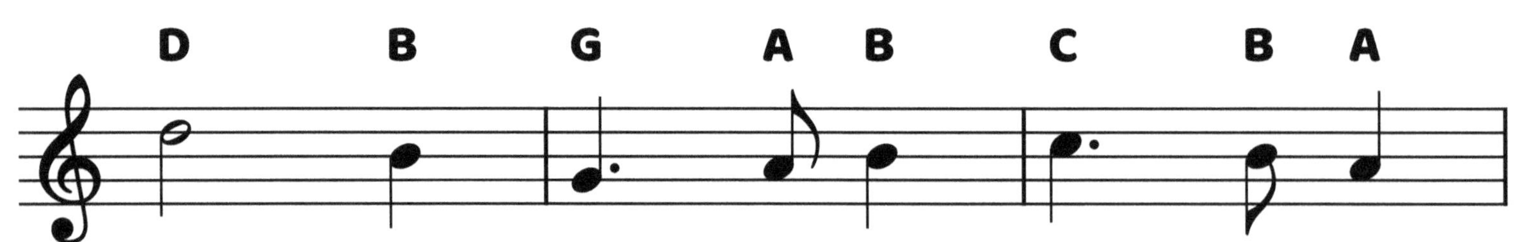

G# F# G# A A G

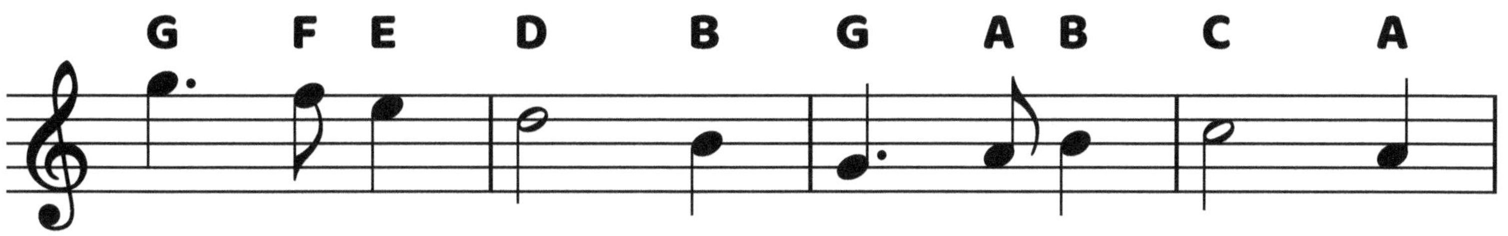
G F E D B G A B C A

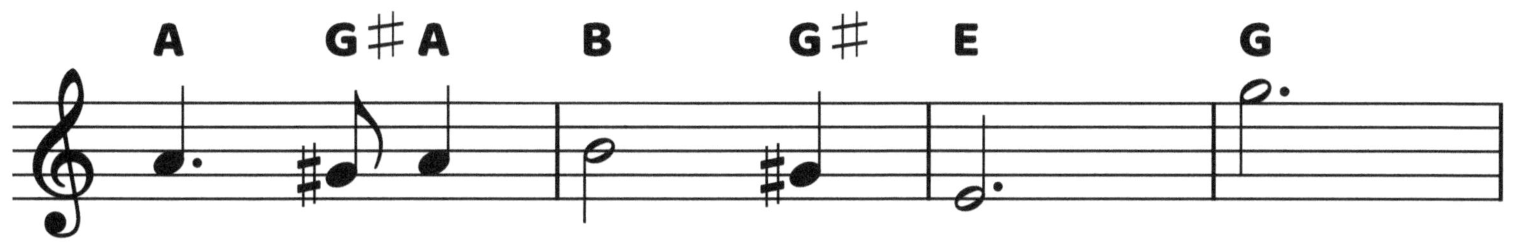
A G# A B G# E G

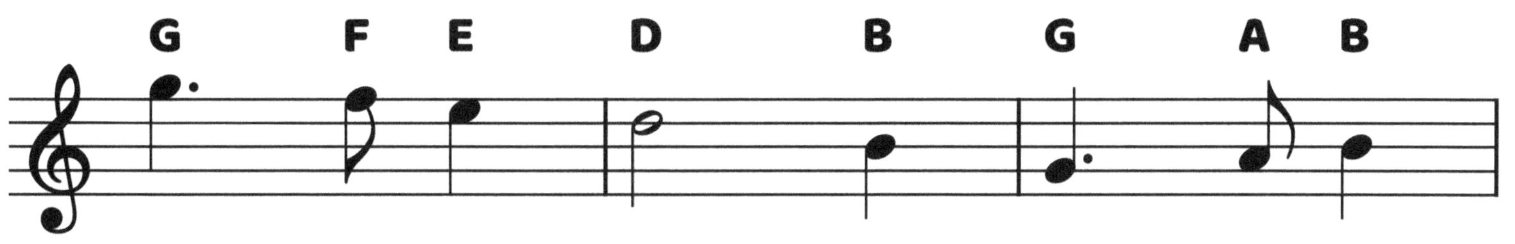
G F E D B G A B

C B A G# F# G# A A

Heads and Shoulders Knees and Toes

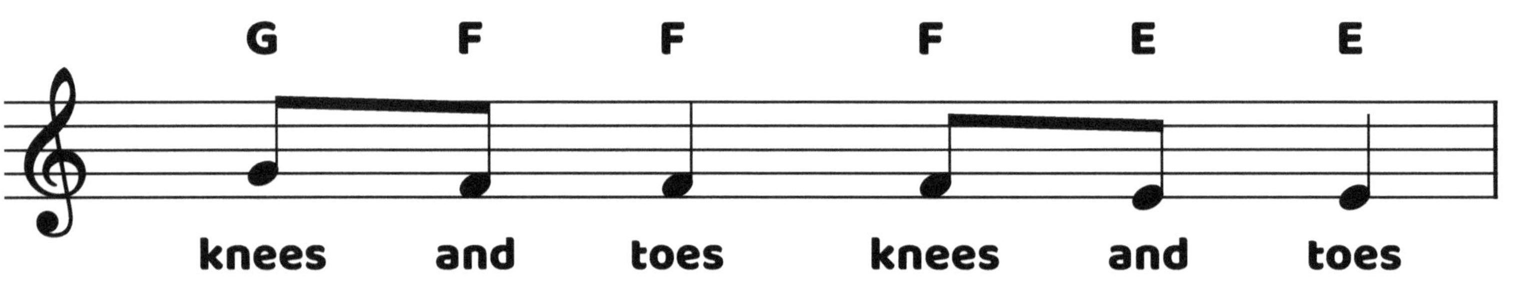

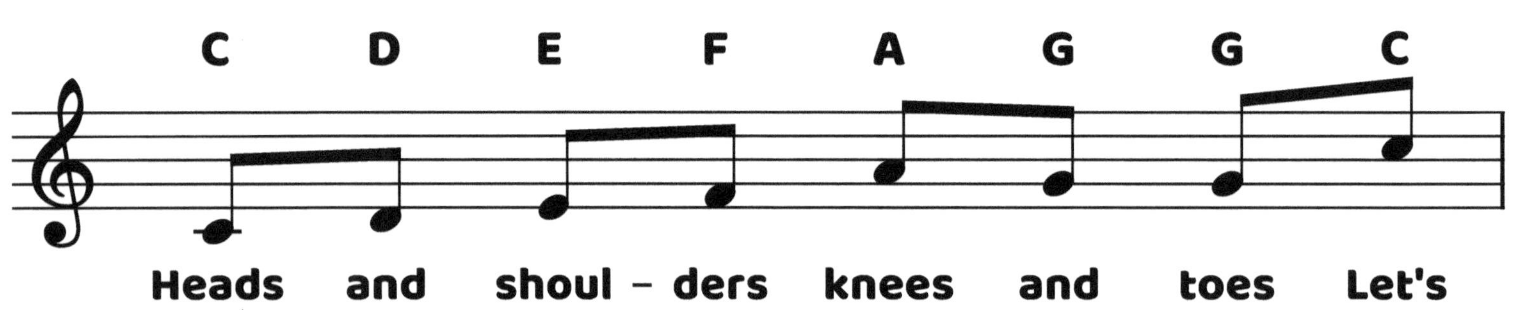

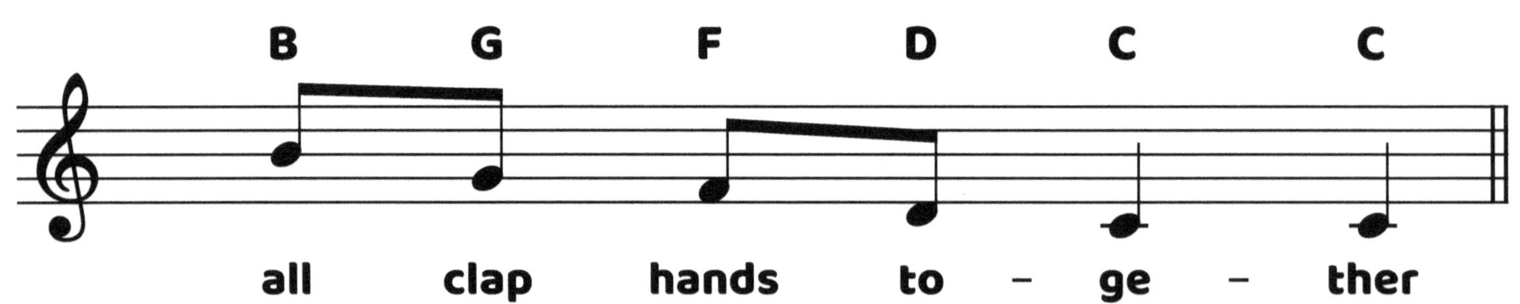

12

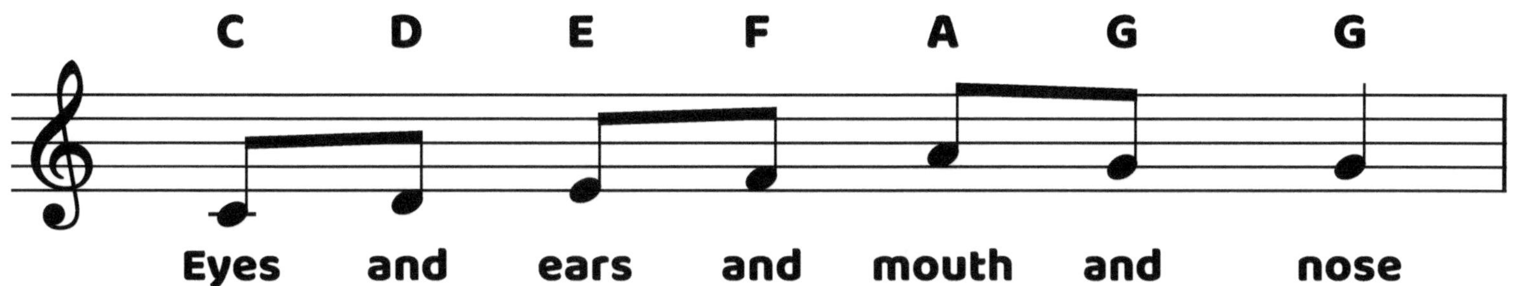

C D E F A G G
Eyes and ears and mouth and nose

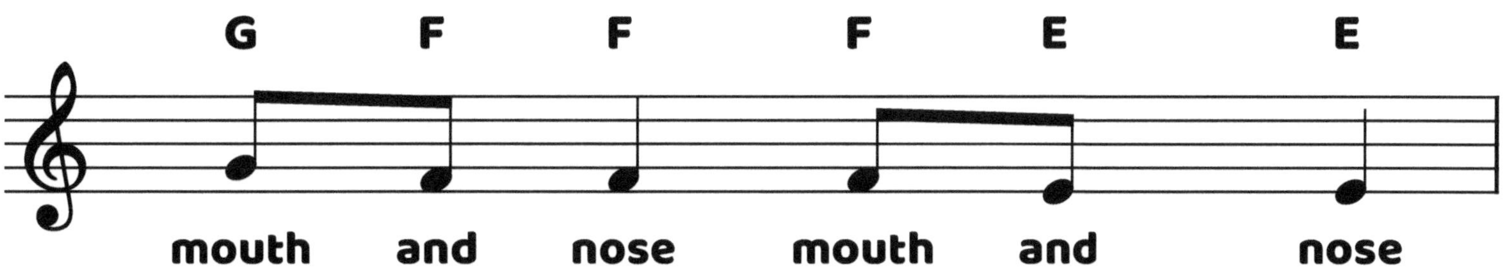

G F F F E E
mouth and nose mouth and nose

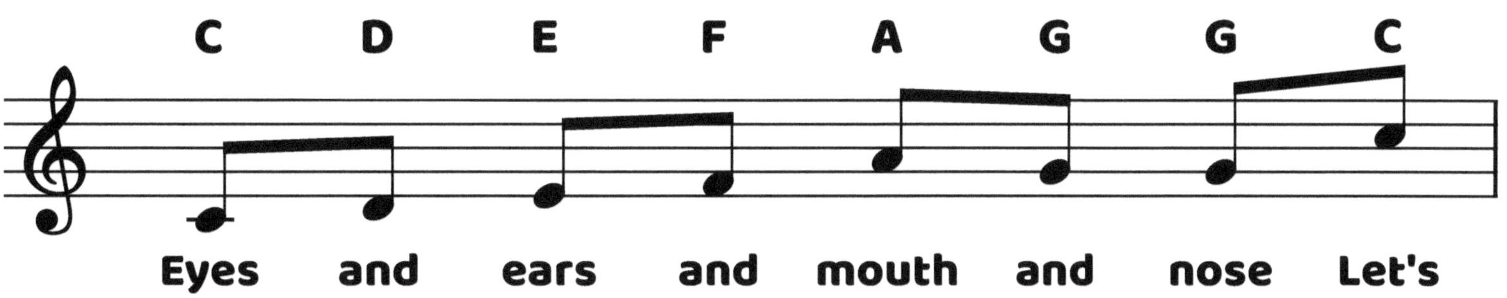

C D E F A G G C
Eyes and ears and mouth and nose Let's

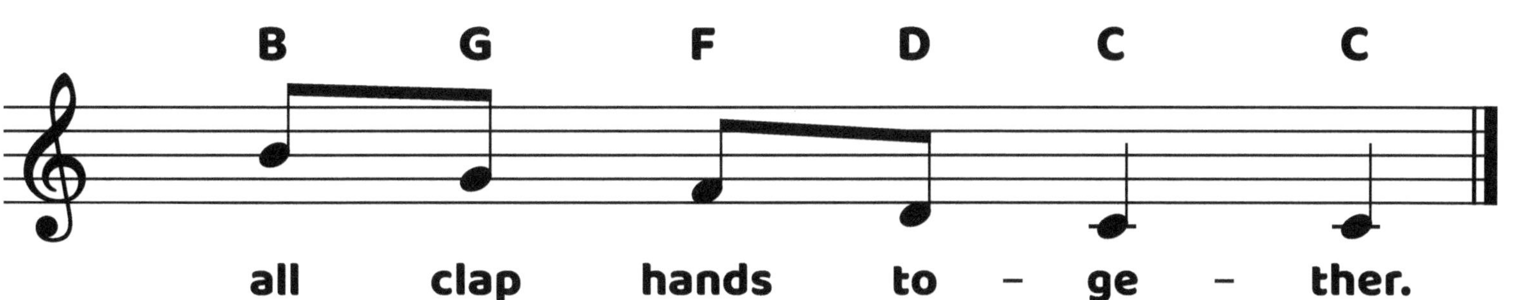

B G F D C C
all clap hands to – ge – ther.

Hickory Dickory Dock

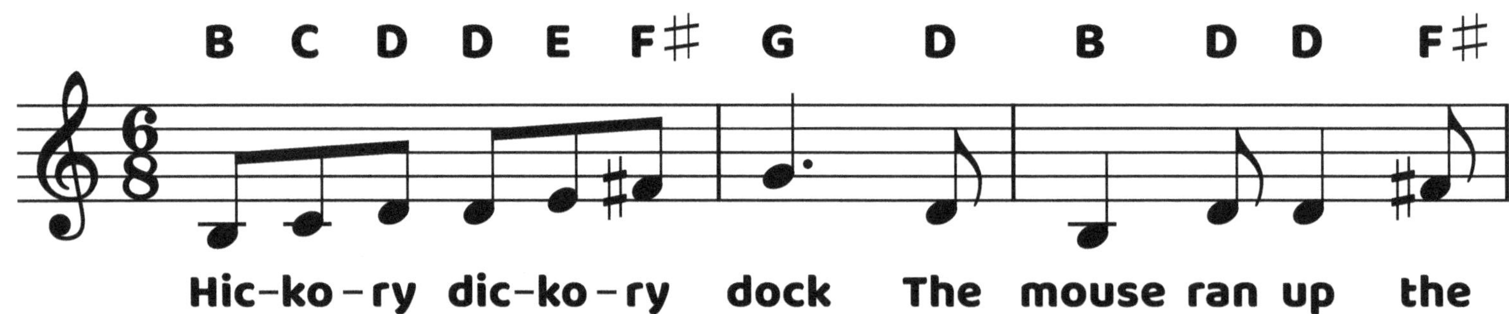

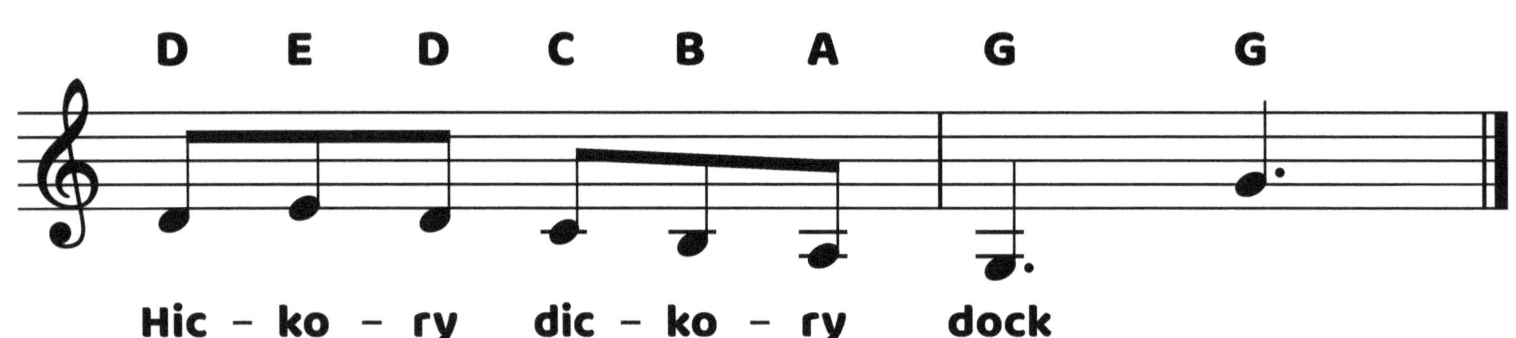

Humpty Dumpty

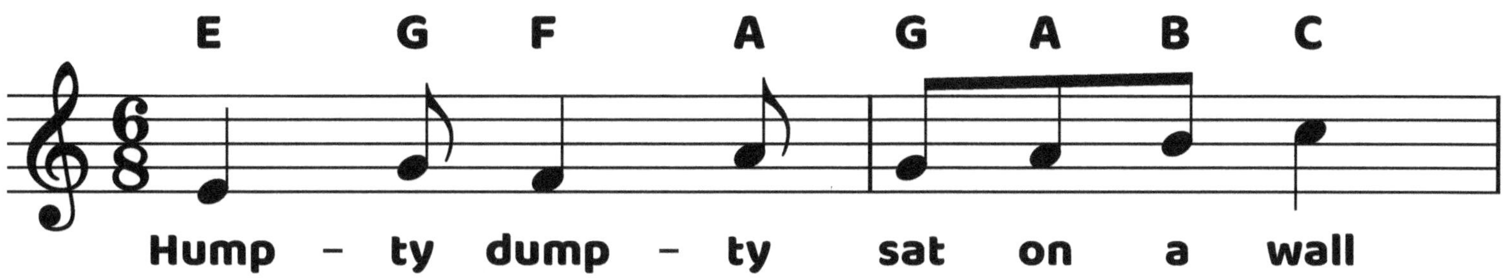

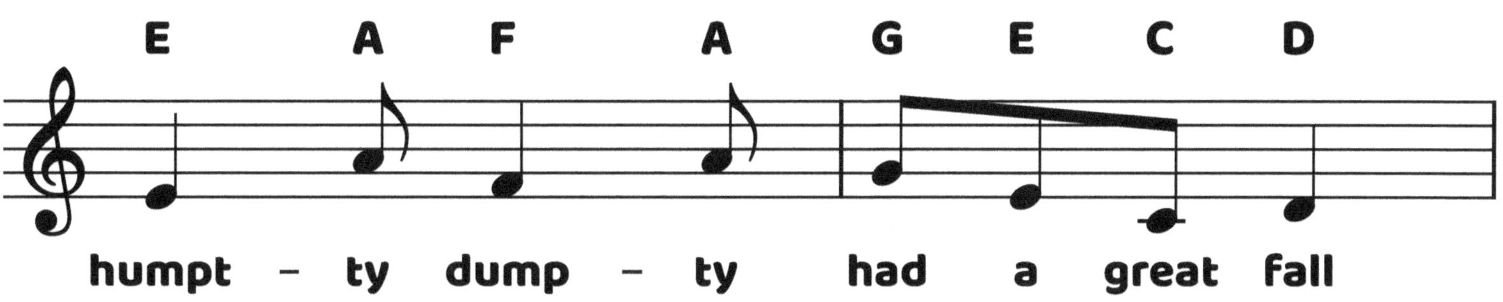

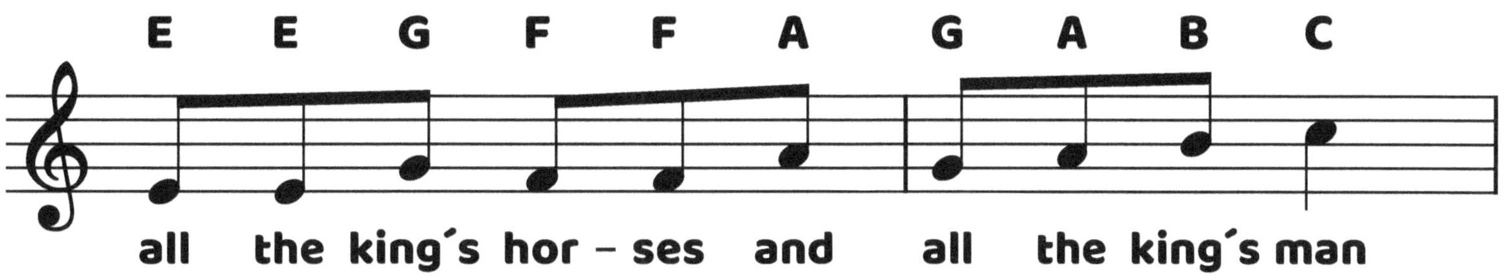

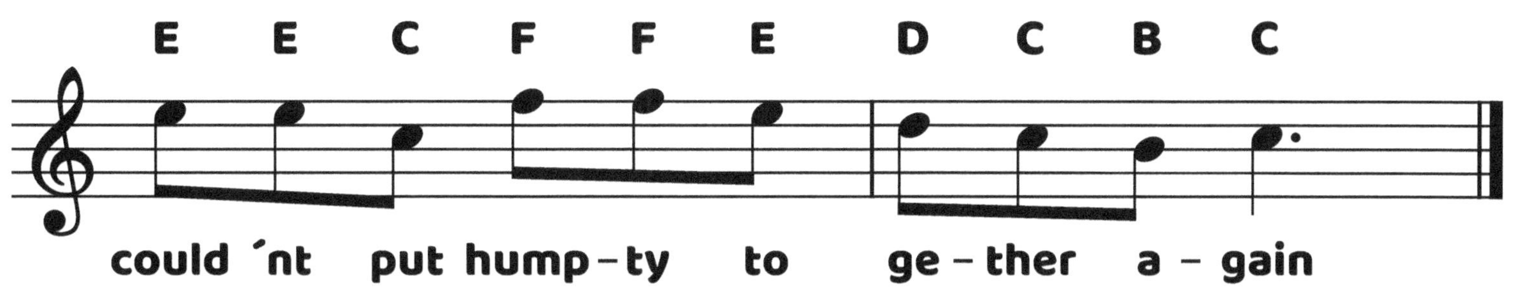

I Gave My Love a Cherry (The Riddle Song)

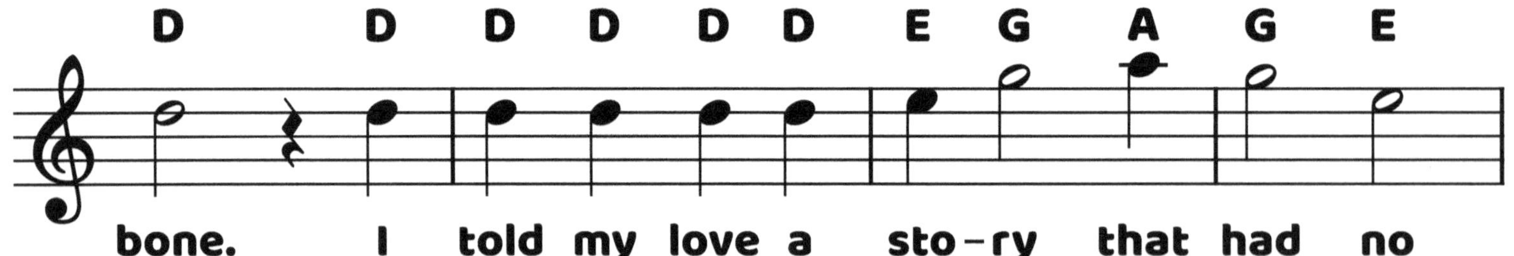

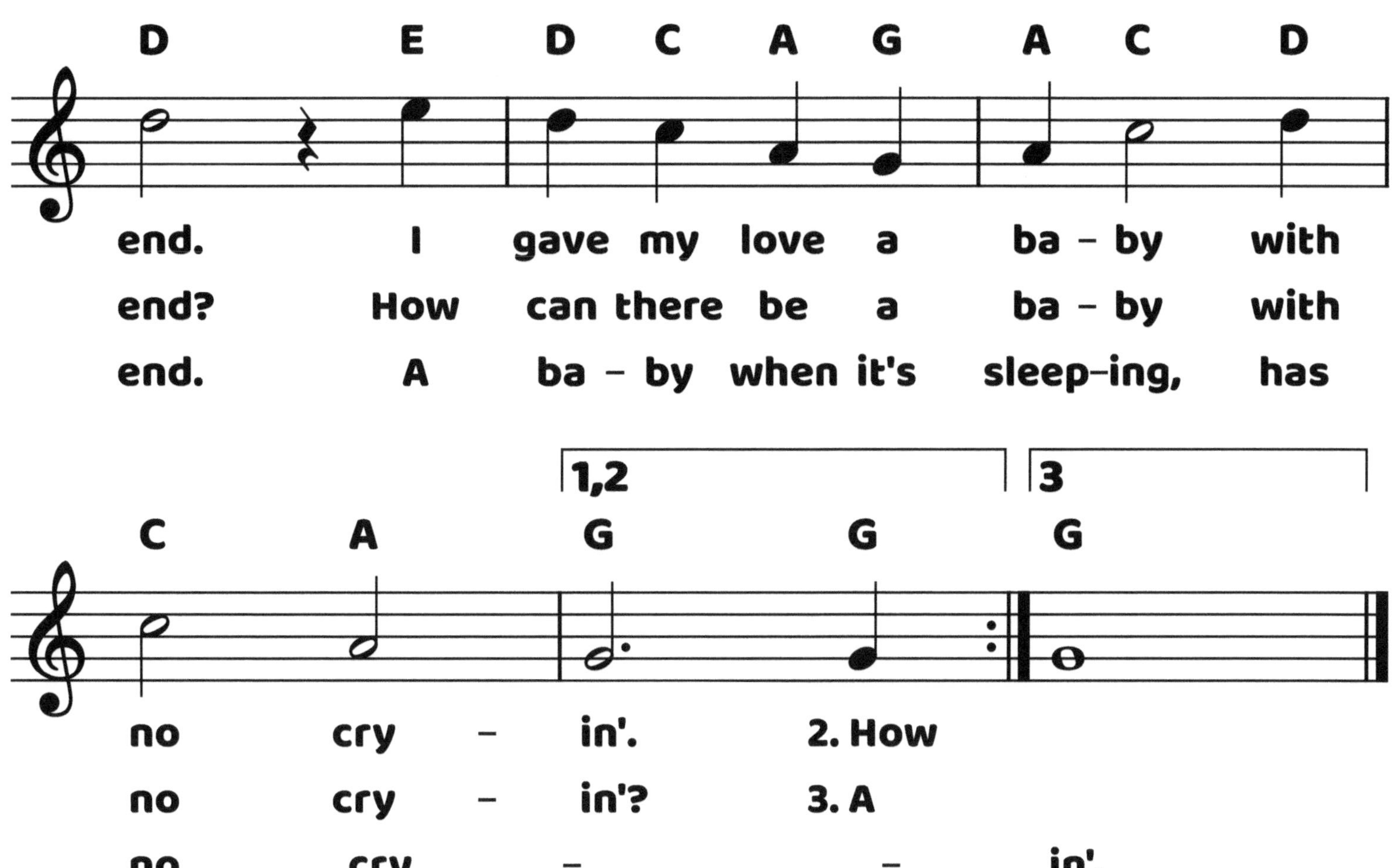

D   E   D   C   A   G   A   C   D
end.   I   gave my love a   ba – by with
end?   How can there be a   ba – by with
end.   A   ba – by when it's sleep–ing, has

1,2   3
C   A   G   G   G
no   cry – in'.   2. How
no   cry – in'?   3. A
no   cry –   –   in'.

Joy to the World

London Bridge Is Falling Down

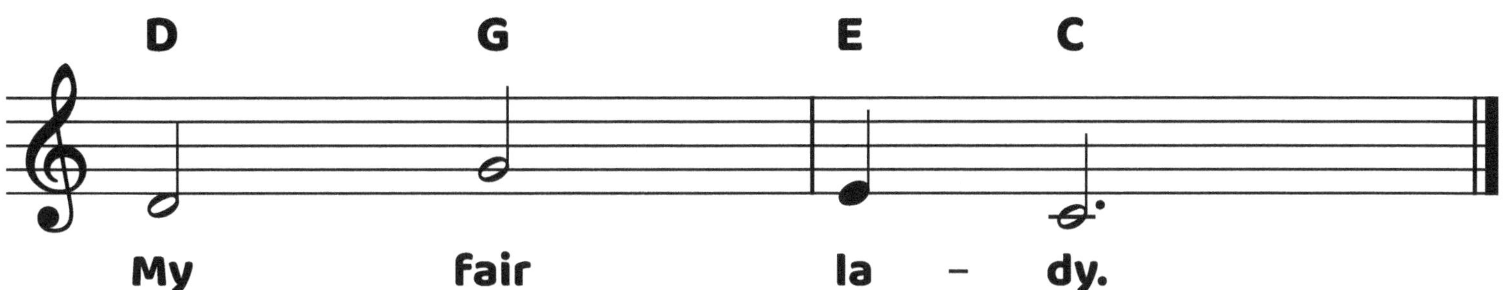

Mozart Quaternário-2 (8/8)

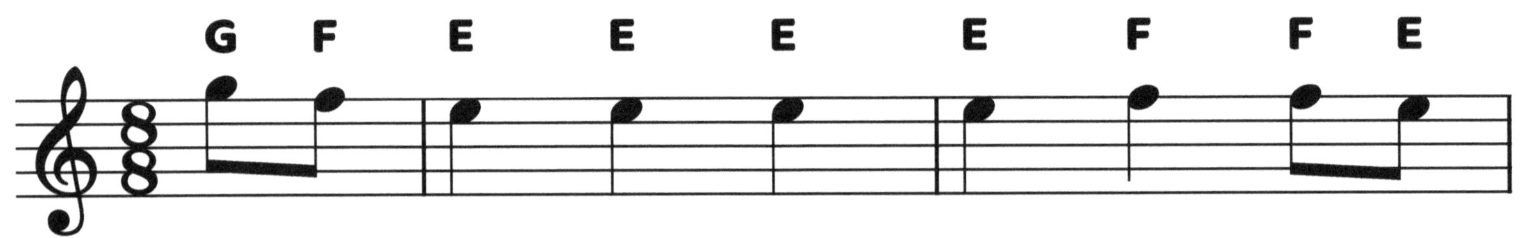

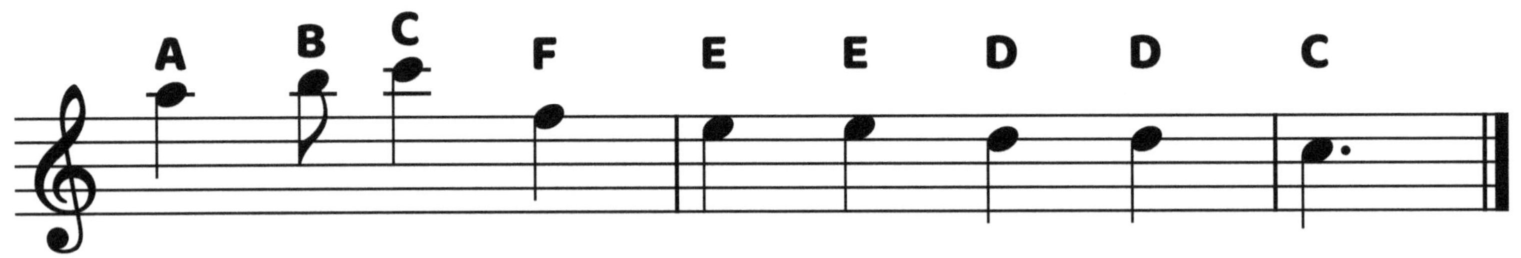

One Little Finger

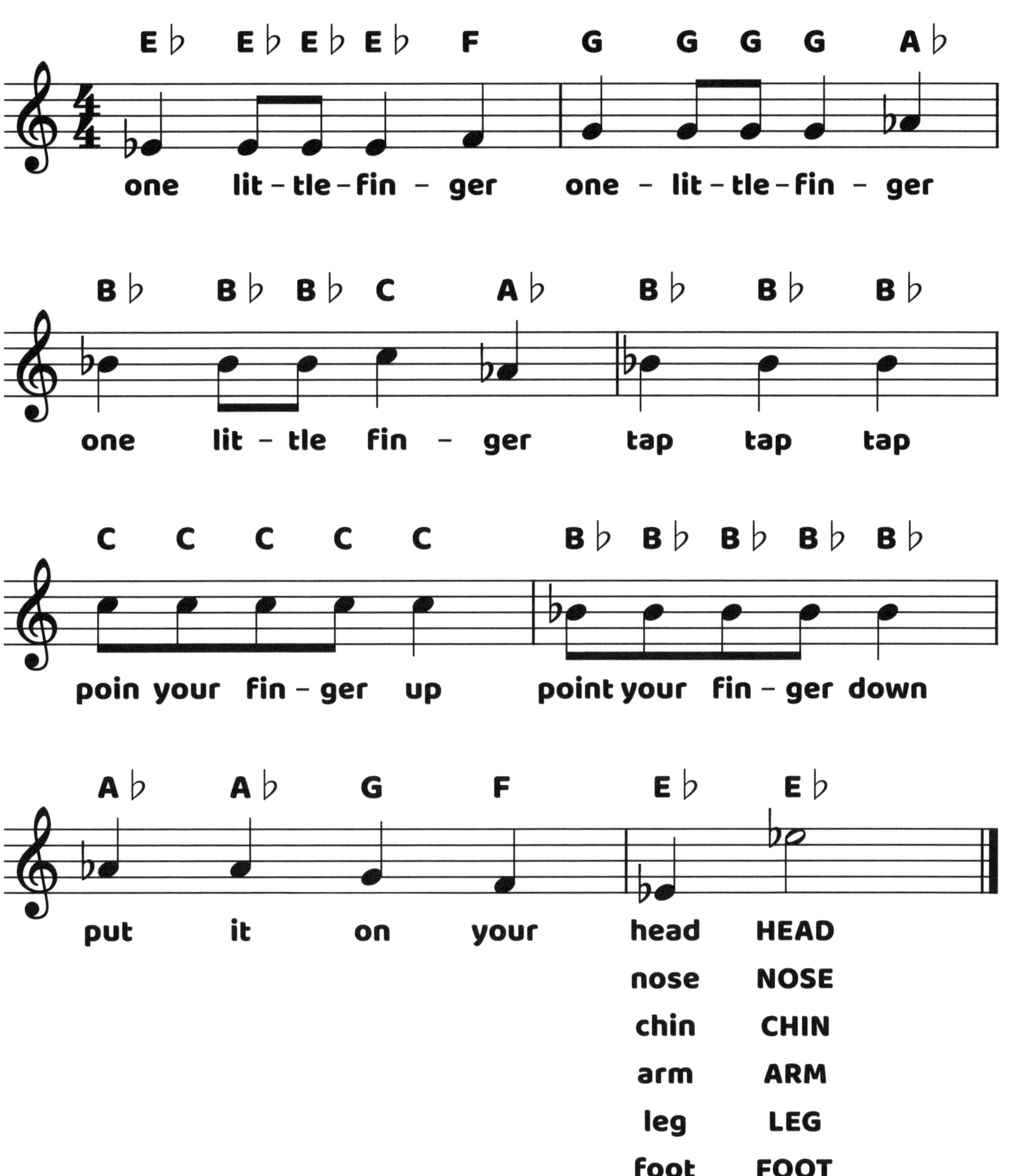

Oh My Darling, Clementine

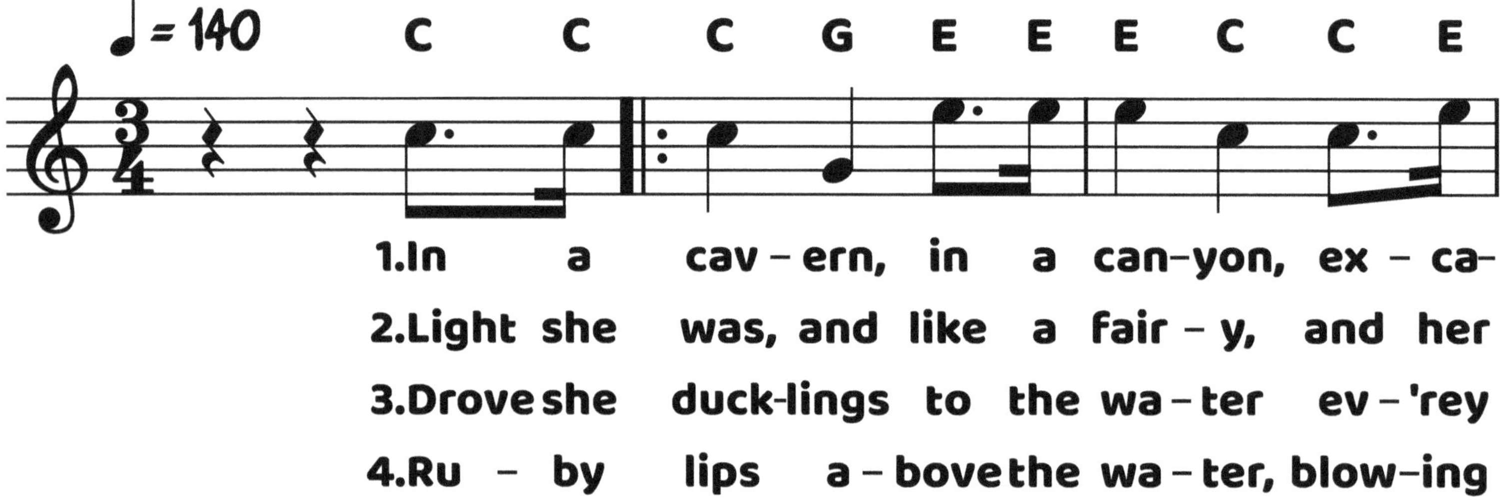

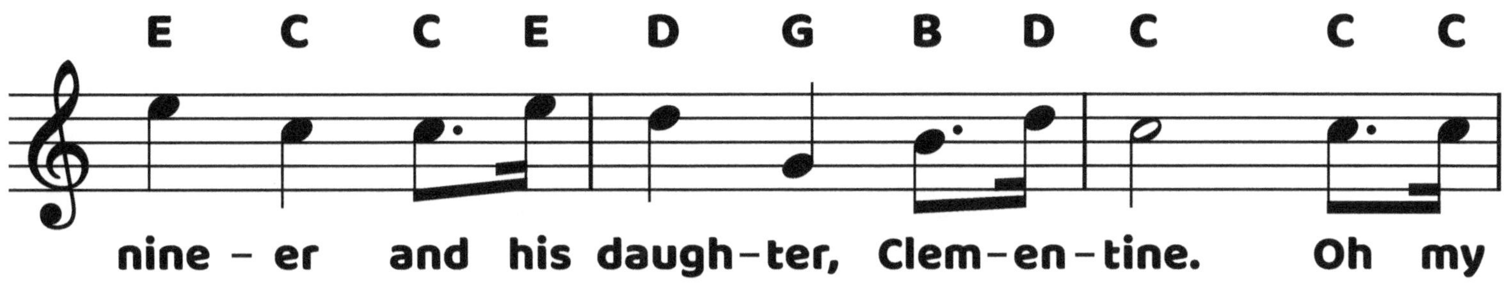

E C C E D G B D C C C
nine – er and his daugh–ter, Clem–en–tine. Oh my
top – ses, san–dals were for Clem–en–tine.
splin – ter, fell in – to the foam–ing brine.
swim – mer, so I lost my Clem–en–tine.

C G E E E C C E G G F E
dar – ling, oh my dar – ling, oh my dar – ling Clem–en–

D D E F F E E♭E C C E
tine. You are lost and gone for–ev – er, dread–ful

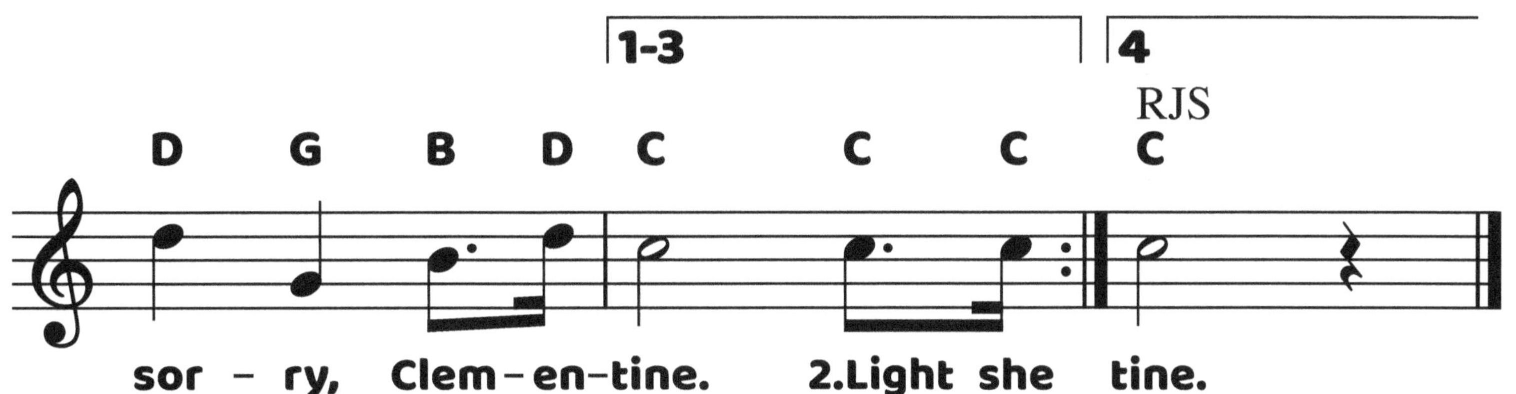

1-3
4
RJS
D G B D C C C C
sor – ry, Clem–en–tine. 2.Light she tine.
3.Drove she
4.Ru – by

Oh! Dem Golden Slippers

F Si♭ D C Si♭ F G C E♭ D C G
Oh, them gold-en slip-pers Oh, them gold-en slip-pers

A A A A Si♭ C C C A Si♭ A Si♭ C
gold-en slip-pers I'm going to wear be – cause they look so

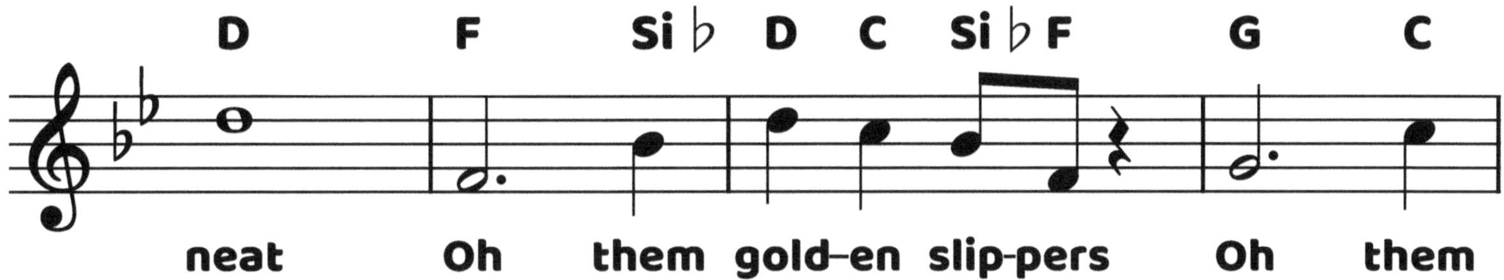

D F Si♭ D C Si♭ F G C
neat Oh them gold–en slip-pers Oh them

E♭ D C G A A A A Si♭ C C E♭ E♭
gold-en slip-pers gold-en slip-pers i'm going to wear to

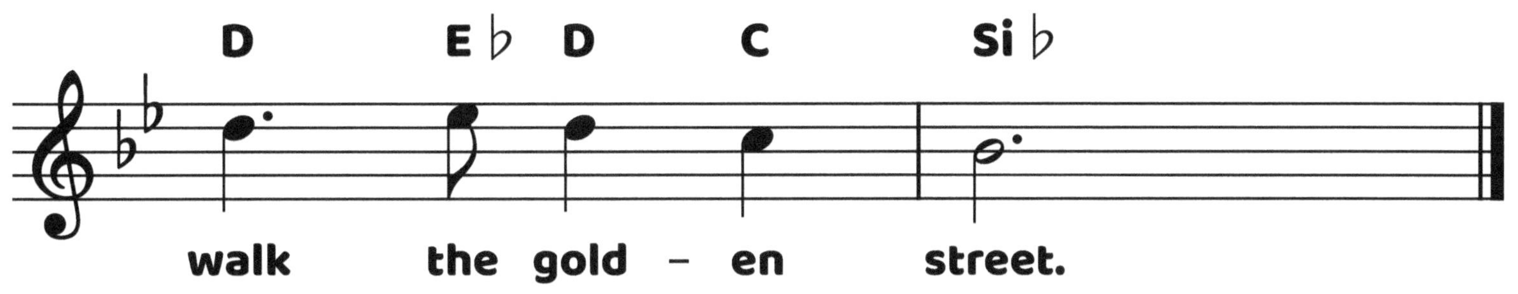

D E♭ D C Si♭
walk the gold – en street.

Oh! You Beautiful Doll

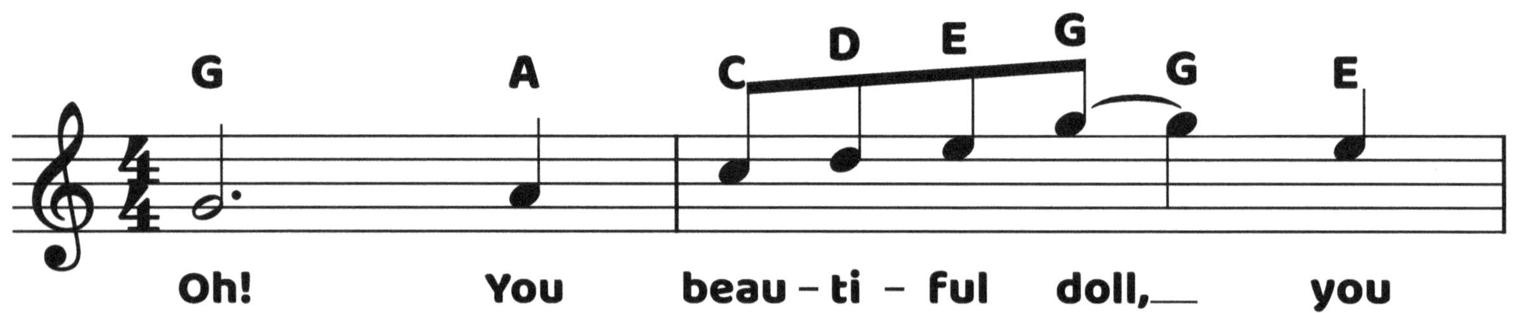

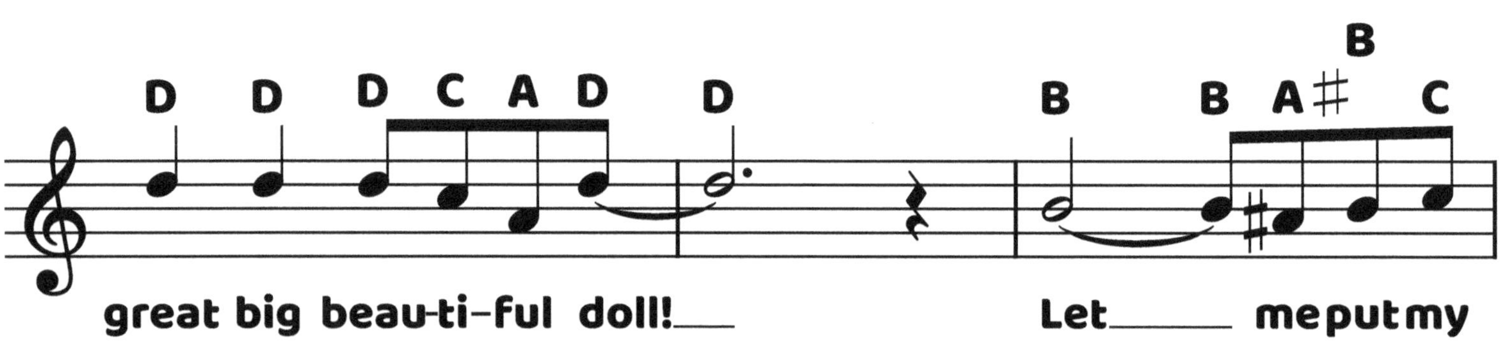

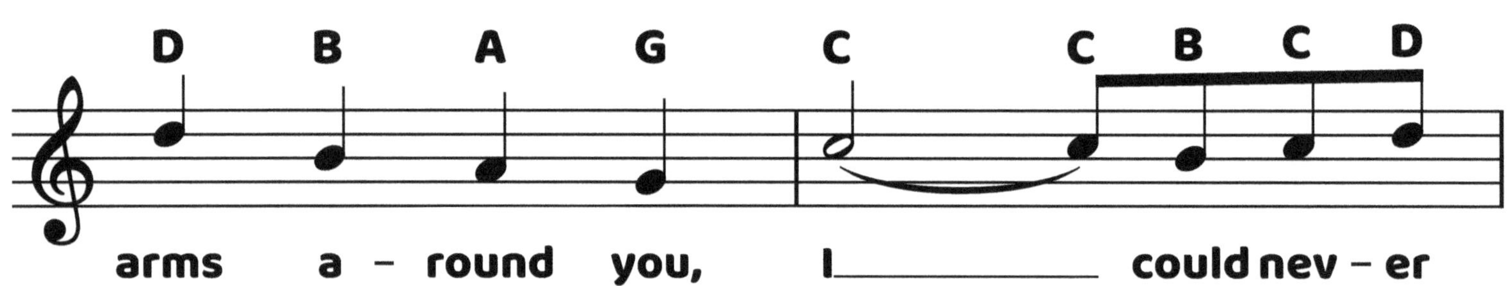

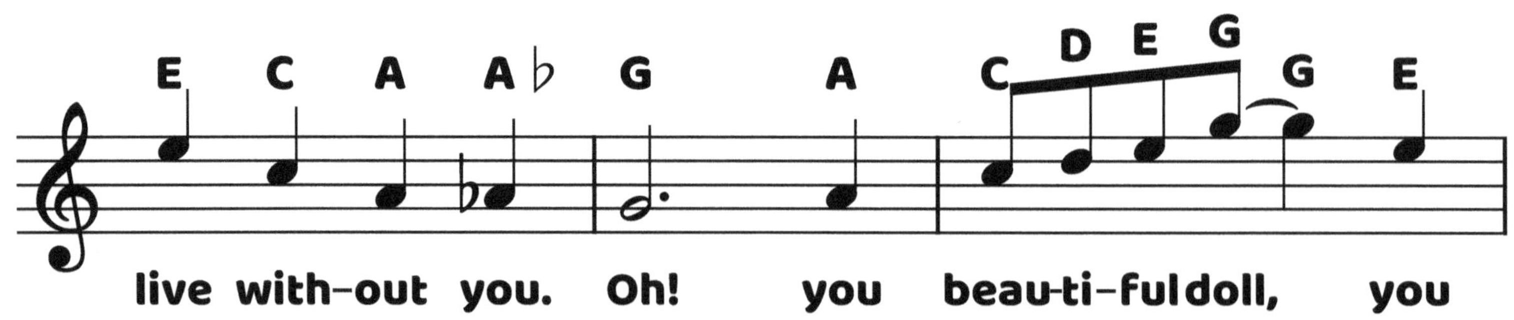

D D D C A D D C D
great big beau ti - ful doll!___ If you

E D# E E D C D E D# E E C
ev – er leave me, how my heart would ache, I

E♭ D E♭ E♭ ♭D C D E♭ D E♭ E♭ E E
want to hug you but I fear you'd break. Oh! oh!

E E E E G G E D C
oh! oh! Oh!, you beau - ti ful doll!

Pop! Goes the Weasel

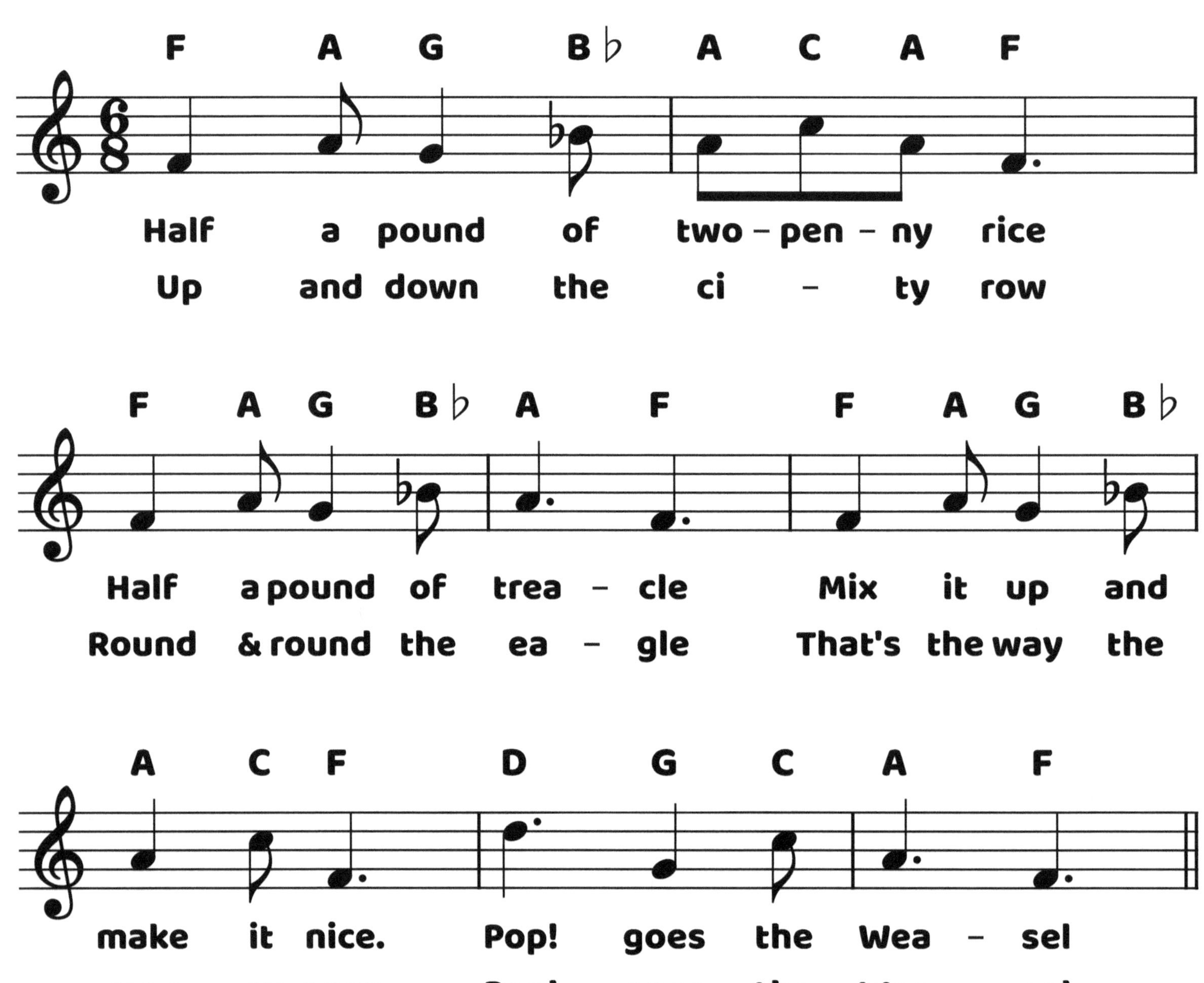

Rain, Rain, Go Away

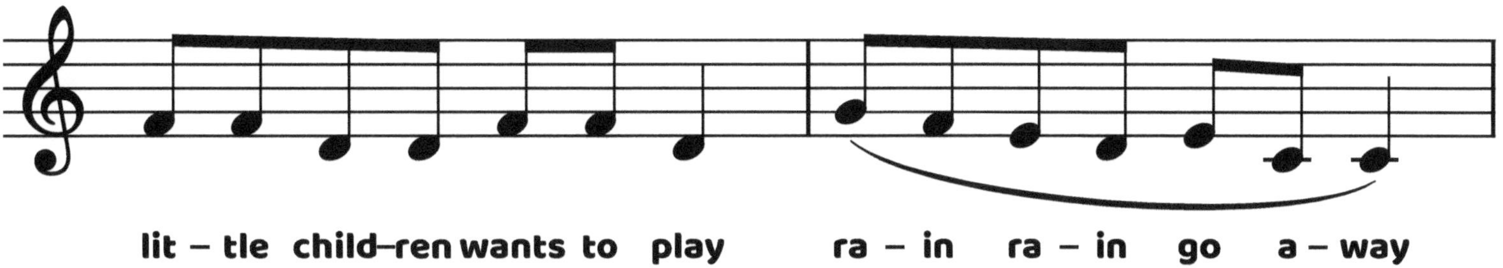

Ring Around the Rosie

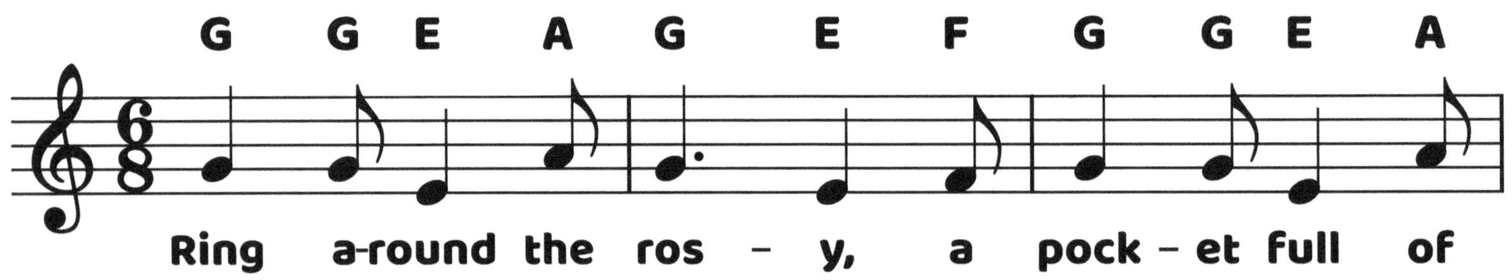

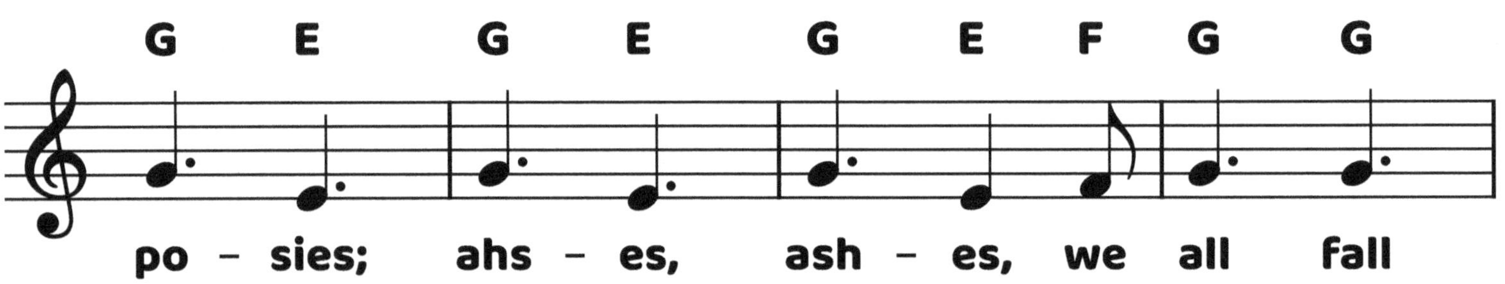

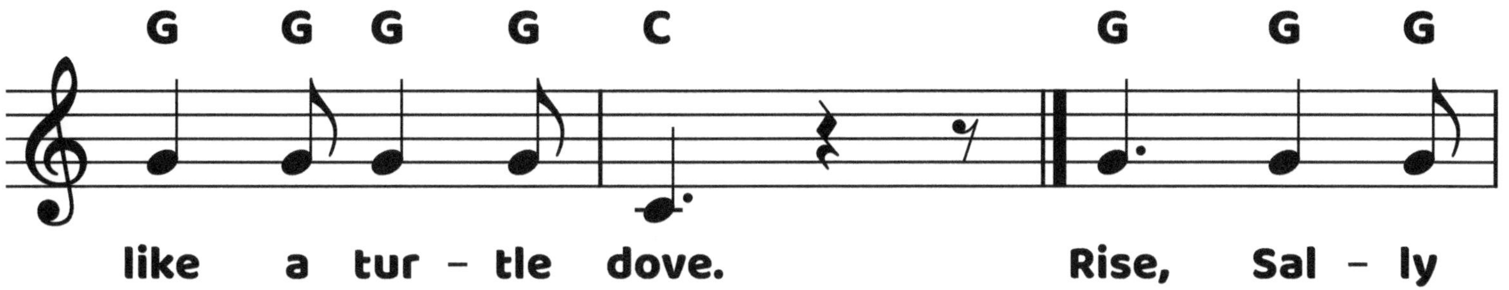
G G G G C G G G
like a tur - tle dove. Rise, Sal - ly

G E G G E A G E G G G
rise, wipe your weep-ing eyes;__ fly to the

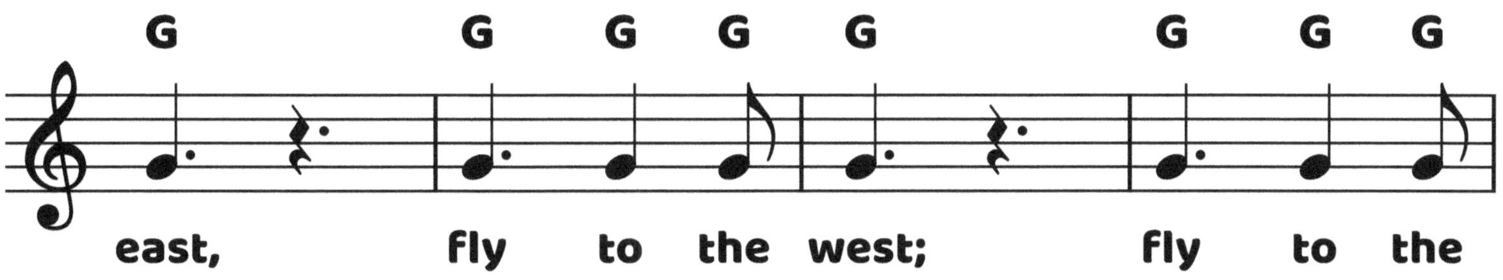
G G G G G G G G
east, fly to the west; fly to the

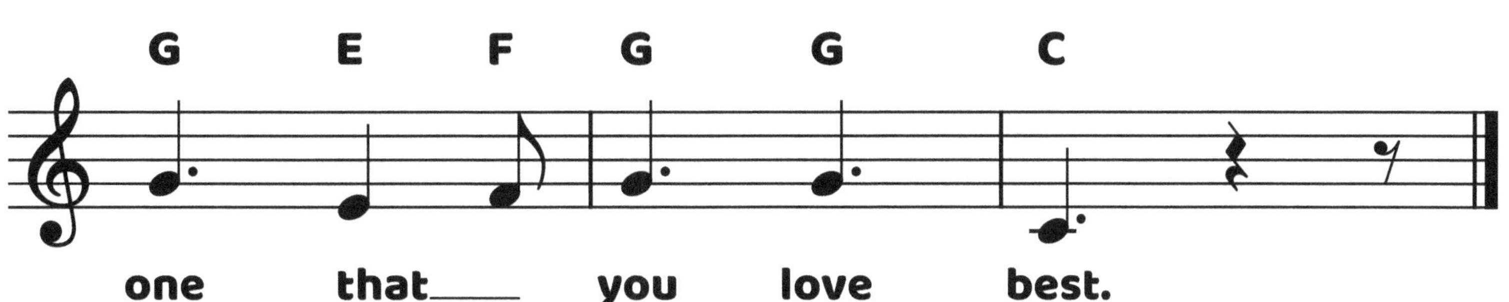
G E F G G C
one that___ you love best.

Row, Row, Row Your Boat

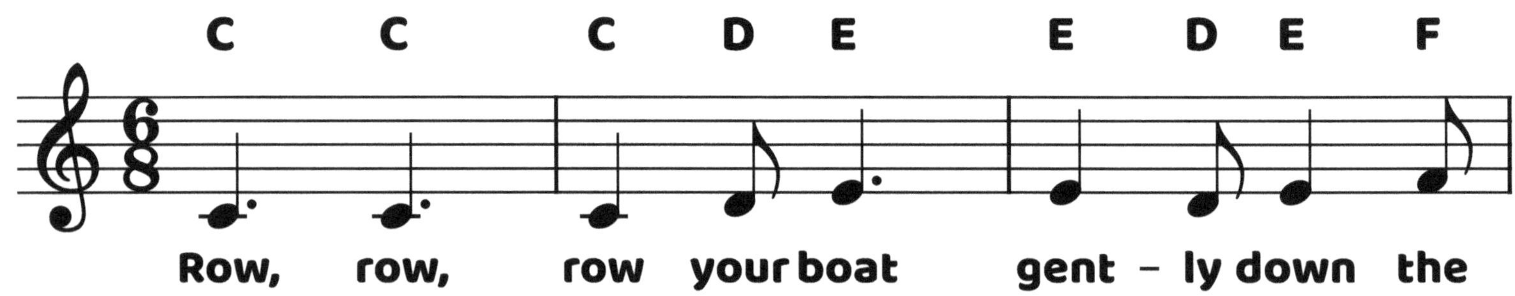

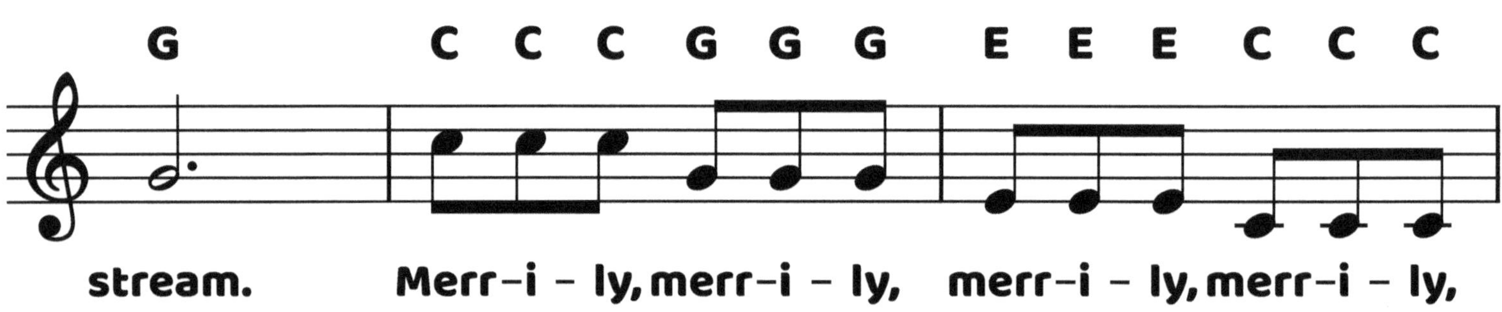

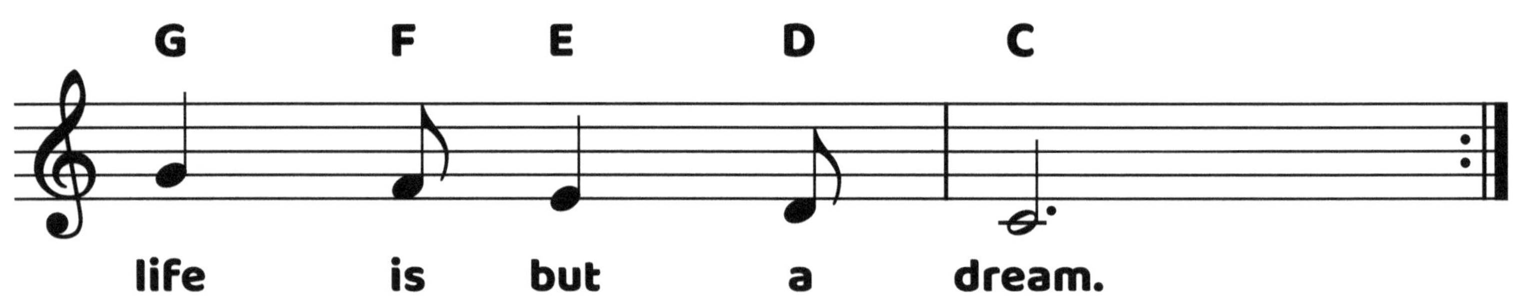

The Mulberry Bush

Shoo Fly, Don't Bother Me

feel, I feel, I feel, I feel, I feel like a morn-in' star.
hear, I hear, I hear, I hear, I hear all the an-gels sing.
1.
2.
D.C. al Fine
star.
Oh,
sing.
Oh,

Silent Night

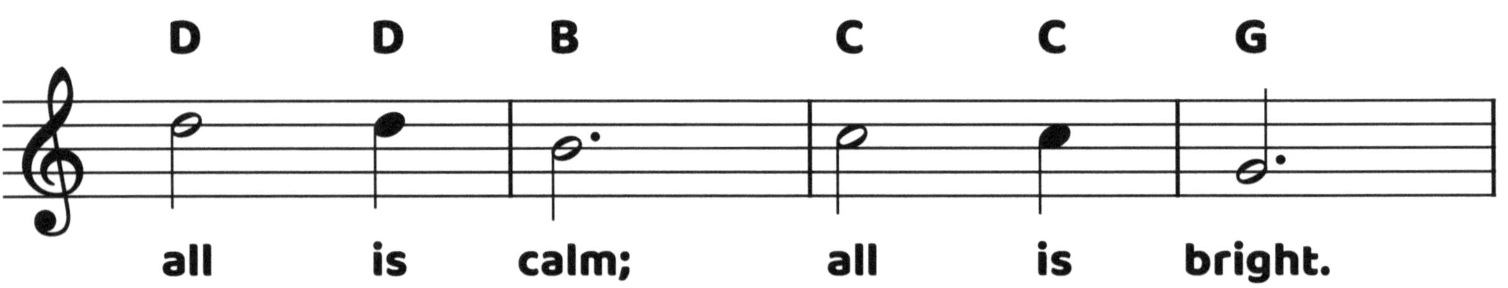

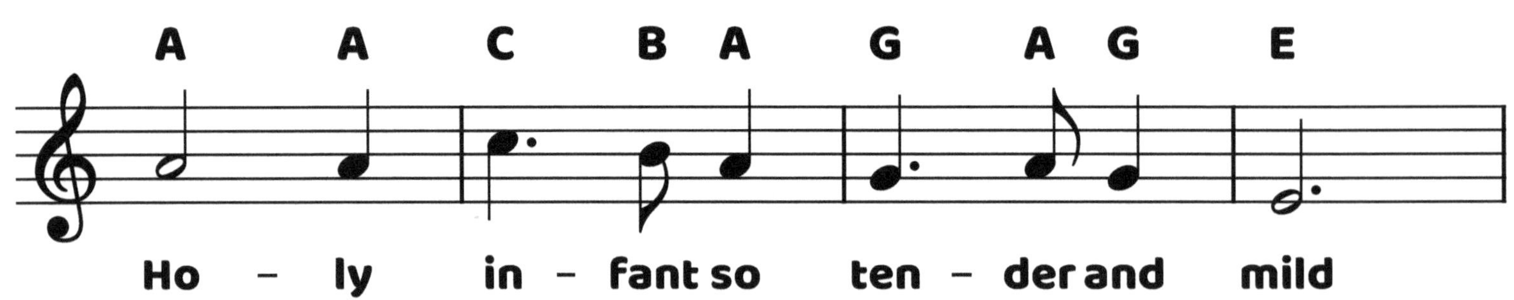

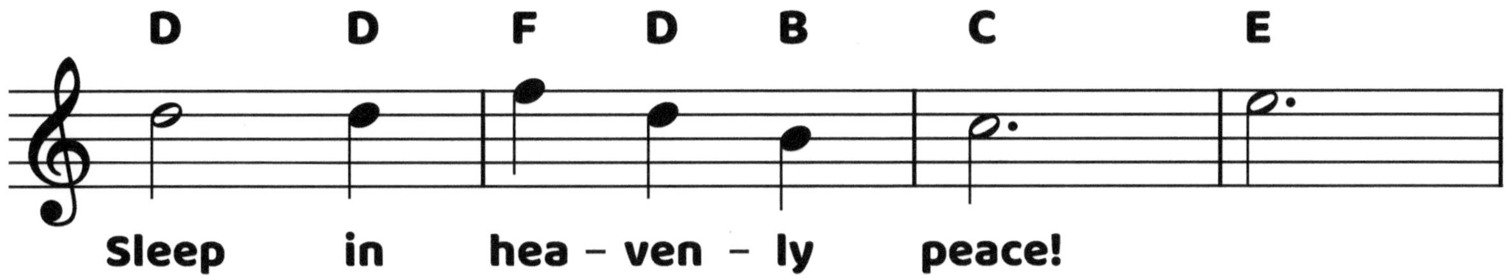

D   D   F   D   B   C   E
Sleep   in   hea – ven – ly   peace!

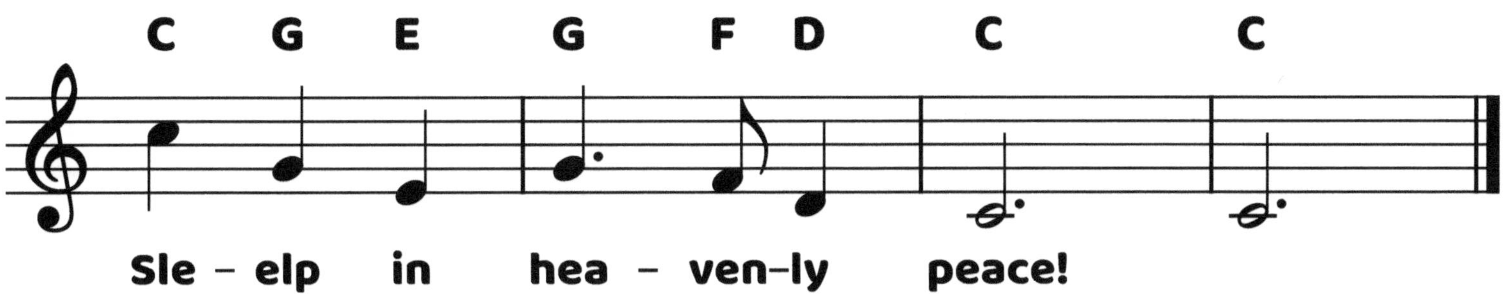

C   G   E   G   F   D   C   C
Sle – elp   in   hea – ven–ly   peace!

Sing a Song of Sixpence

B B D E F F F
Count – ing out his mon – ey. The
F G F D B A
queen was in the par – lor,
G G C D E E E G F G E C C
Eat-ing bread and hon–ey. The maid was in the gar – den,
B B D E F F F G A G F E D E
Hang-ing out the clothes; A – long came a black–bird and
F G A B C
pecked___ off her nose.

Take Me Out to the Ball Game

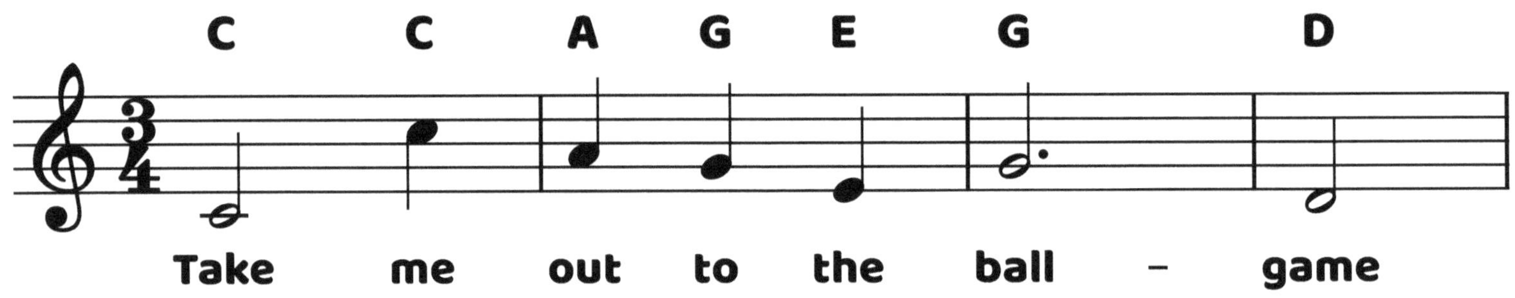

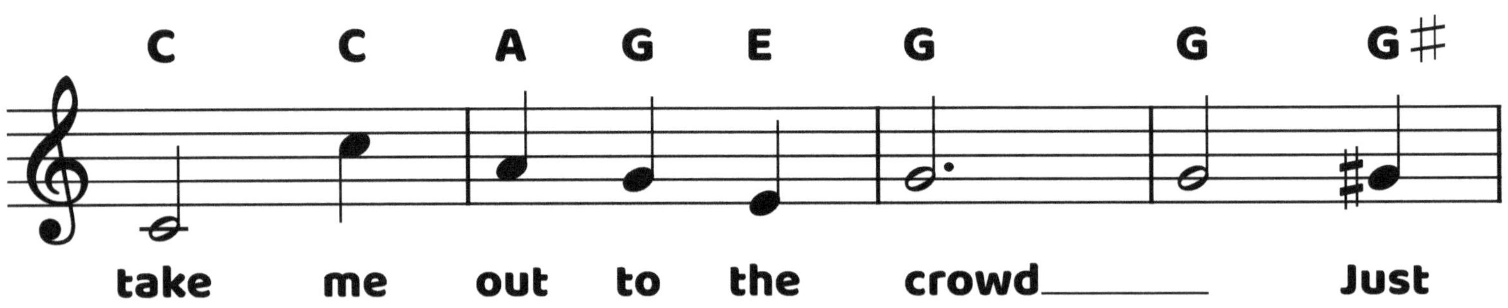

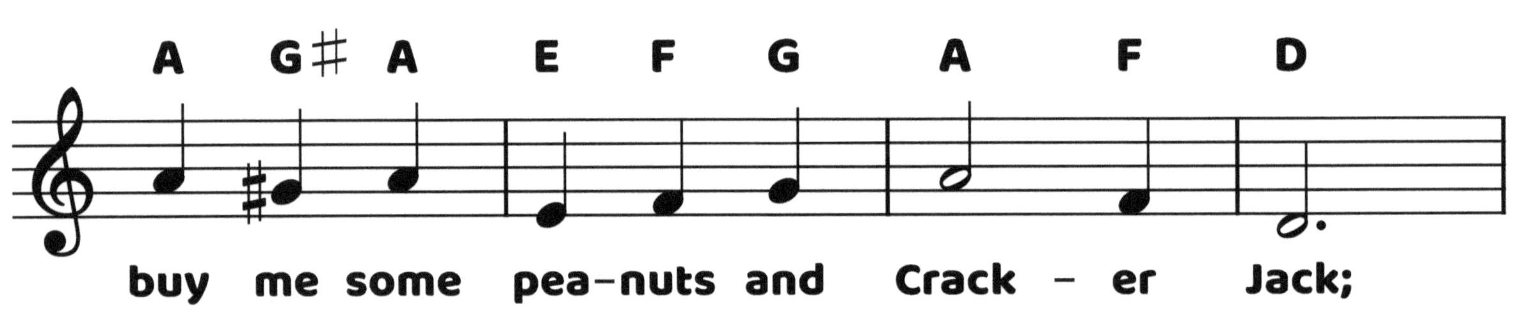

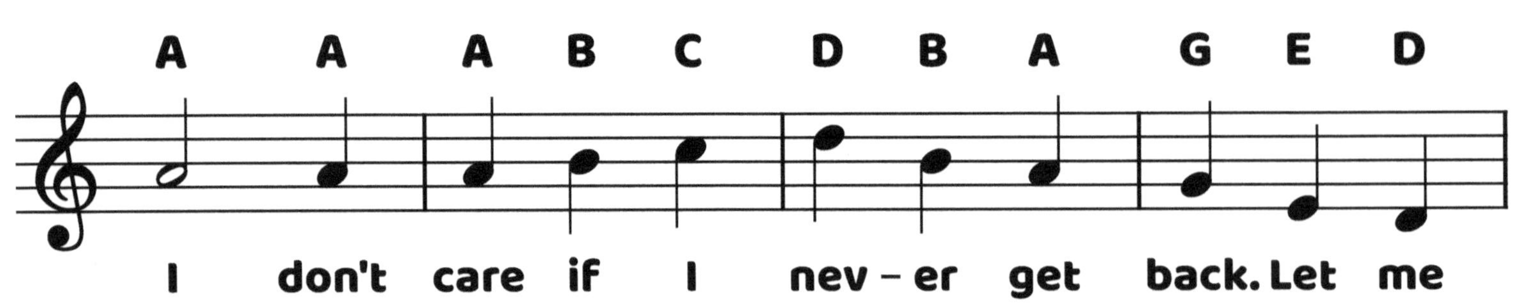

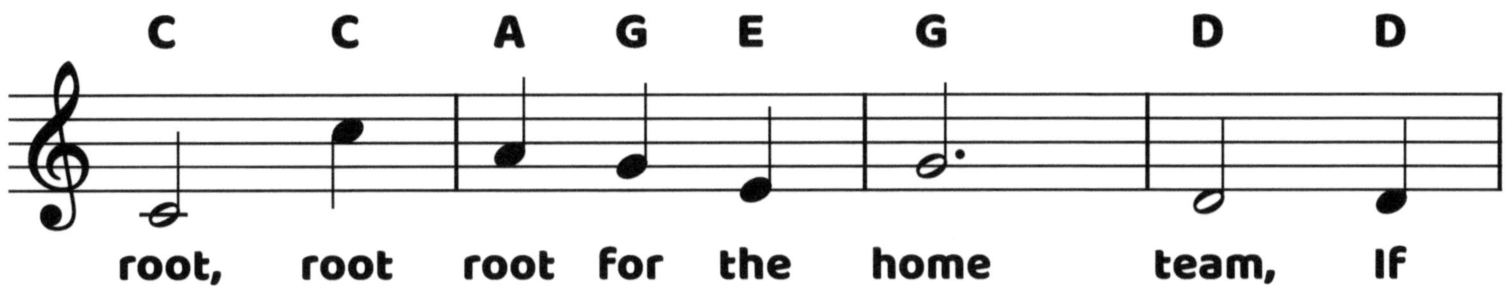

C   C   A   G   E   G   D   D
root, root root for the home team, If

C   D   E   F   G   A   A   B
they don't win, it's a   shame.   For it's

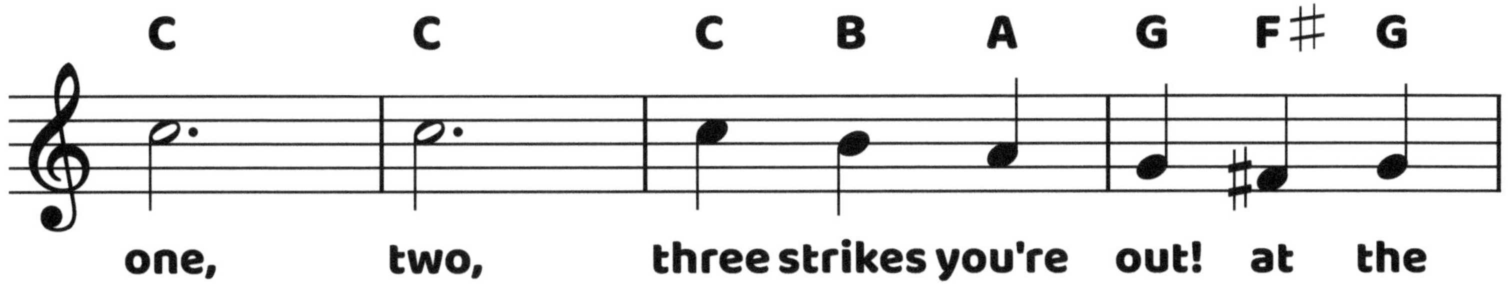

C   C   C   B   A   G   F♯   G
one, two, three strikes you're out! at the

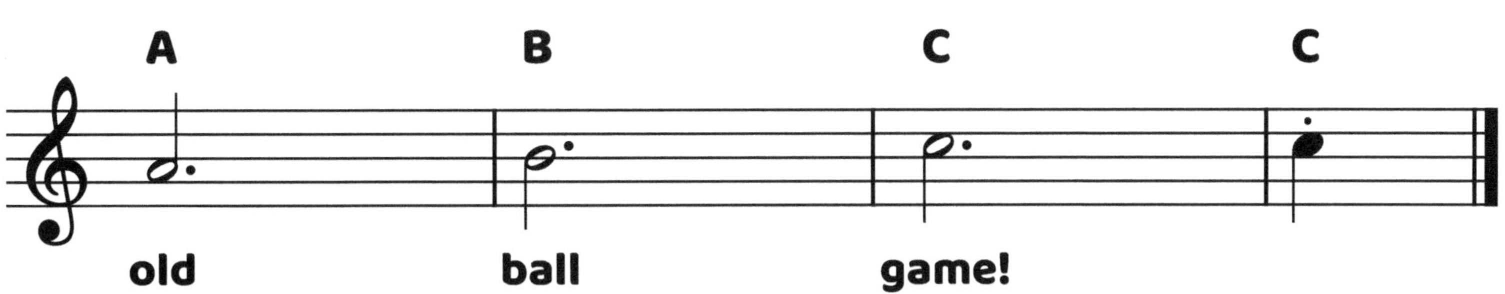

A   B   C   C
old ball game!

The Ants Go Marching

G A B B B A G A A
The ants go mar ching one by
A F# G G G G F# E F# F#
one, the lit tle one stops to such his
F# G A B A G F# E
thumb and they all go mar ching down_
E B B E E B B E E B B E
_ to the ground__ to get out___ of the rain
B C# D#
Boom! Boom! Boom!

The Farmer in the Dell

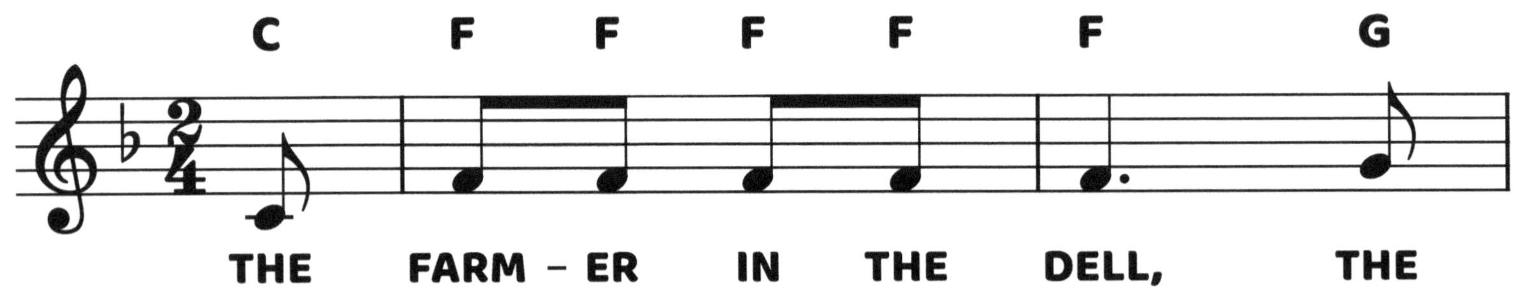

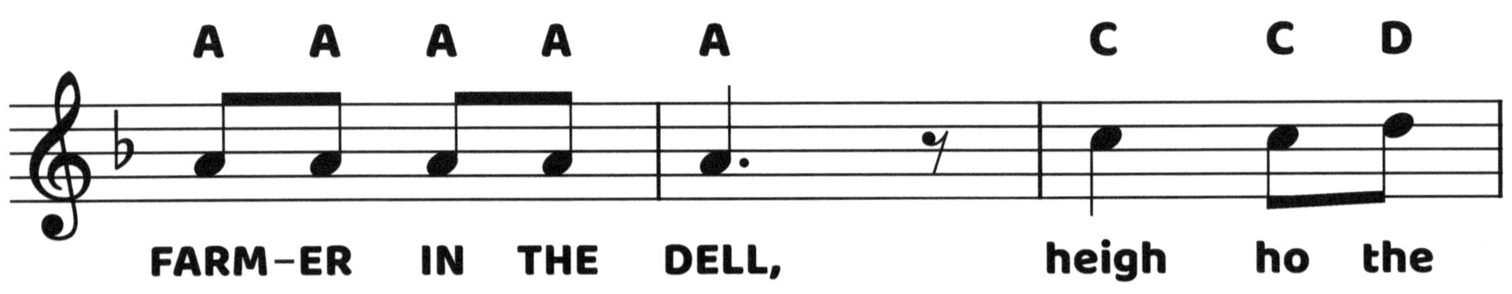

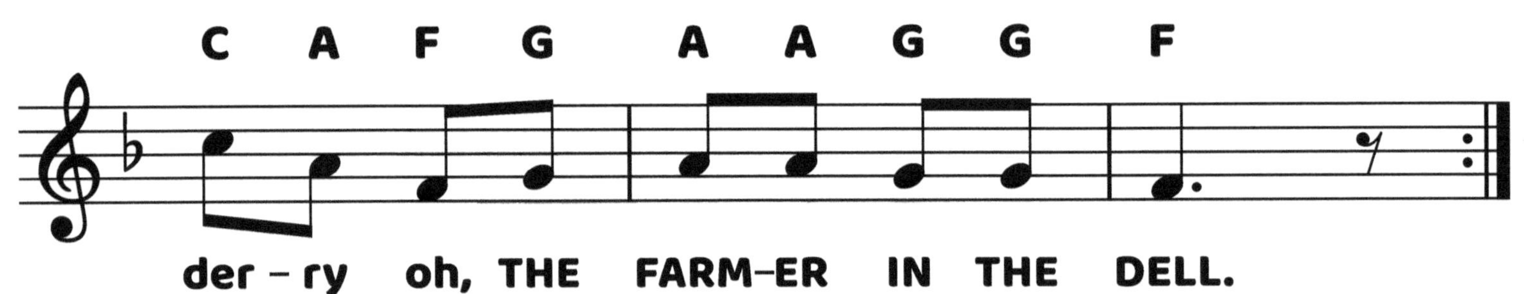

Additional lyrics:

The farmer takes a wife

The farmer takes a wife

Hi-ho, the derry-o

The farmer takes a wife

The wife takes the child...

The child takes the nurse...

The nurse takes the cow...

The cow takes the dog...

The dog takes the cat...

The cat takes the mouse...

The mouse takes the cheese...

The cheese stands alone...

The More We Get Together

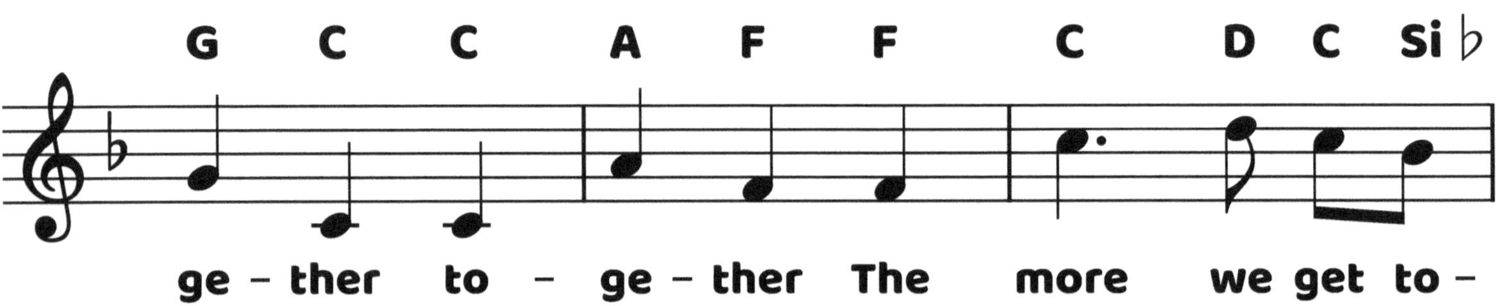

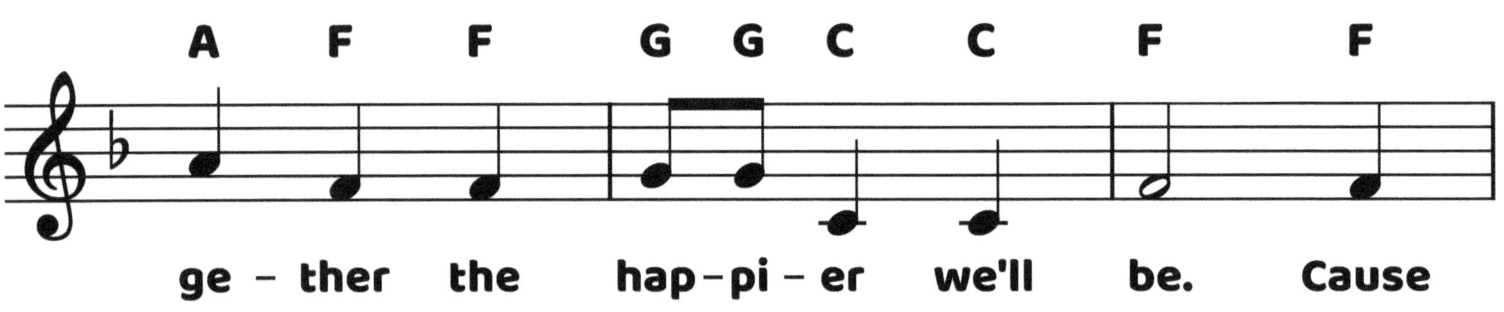

A F F C D C Si♭ A F F
your friends The more we get to – ge – ther the

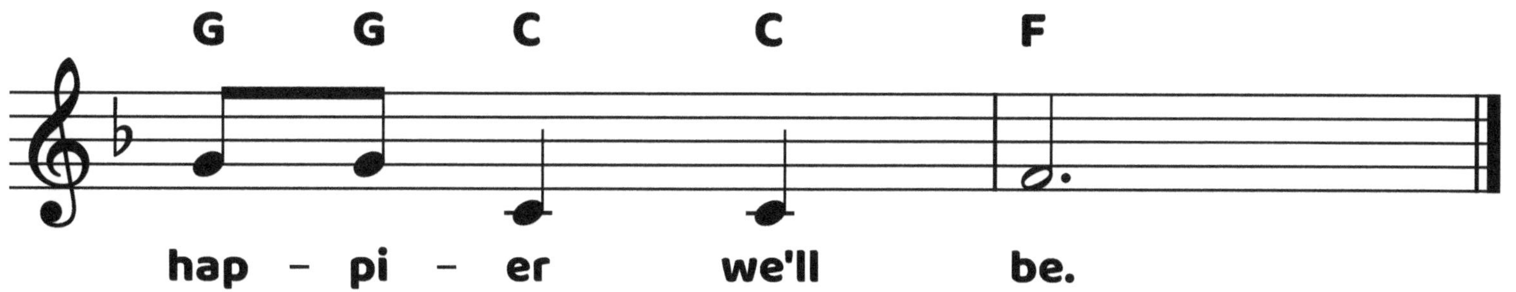

G G C C F
hap – pi – er we'll be.

The Red River Valley

This Little Light of Mine

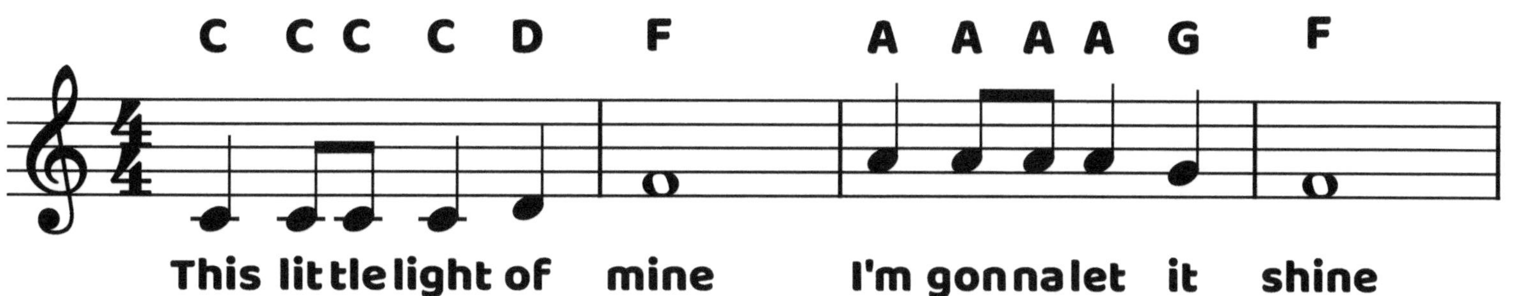

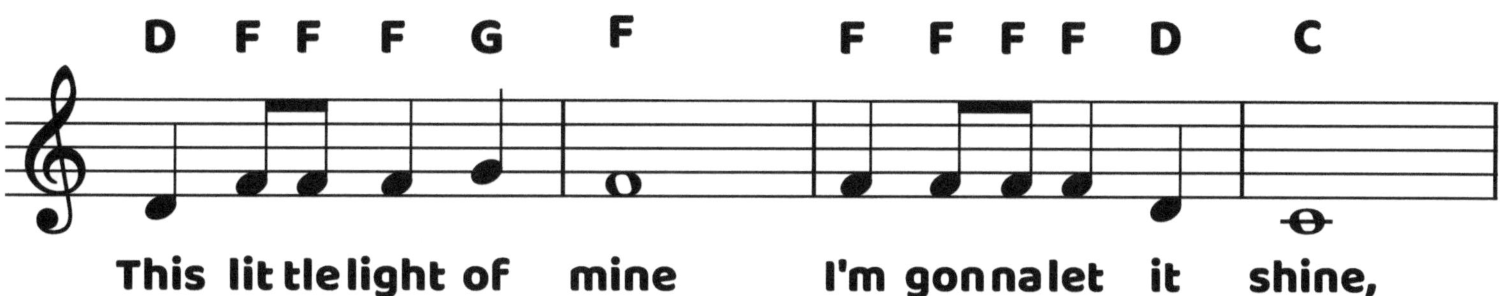

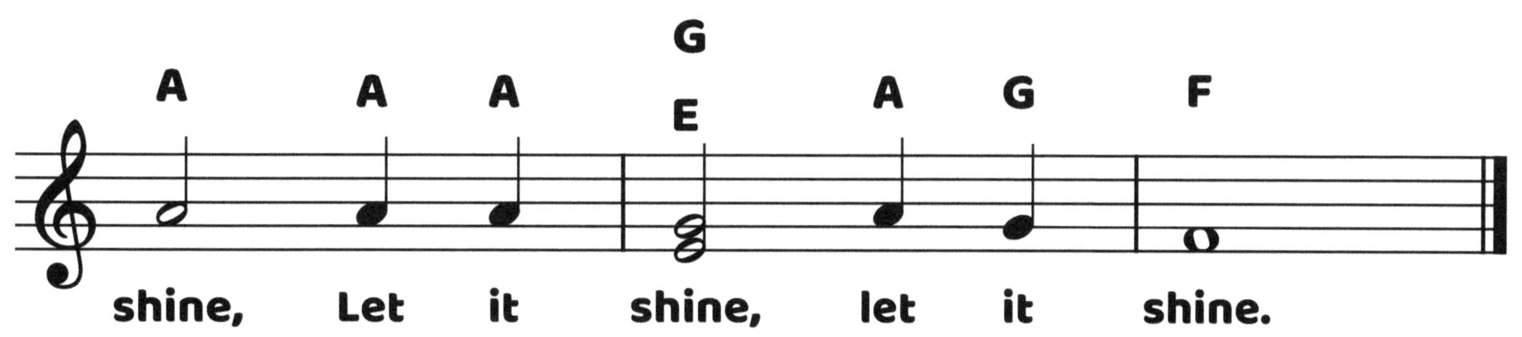

The Yellow Rose of Texas

part. She's the sweet-est lit – tle rose-bud That

Tex – as ev – er knew. Here eyes are bright as

dia-monds, They spark-le like the dew. You

talk a-bout your Di–nah And sing of Ro-sa – lie, The

Yel-low Rose of Tex–as is the on –ly girl for me.

Three Blind Mice

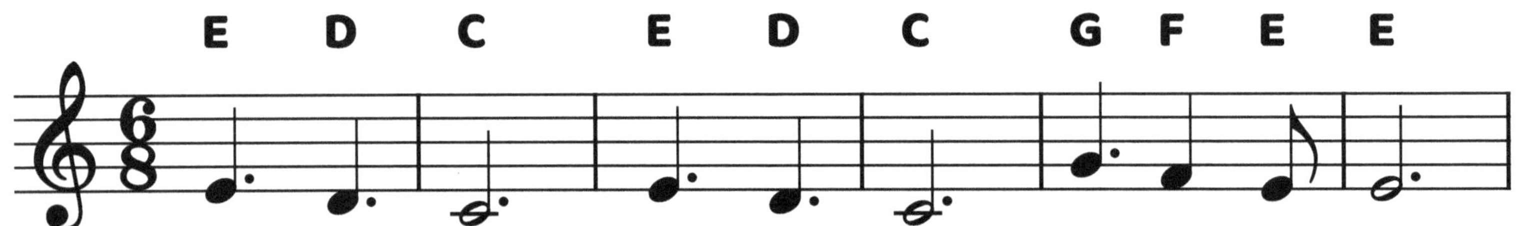

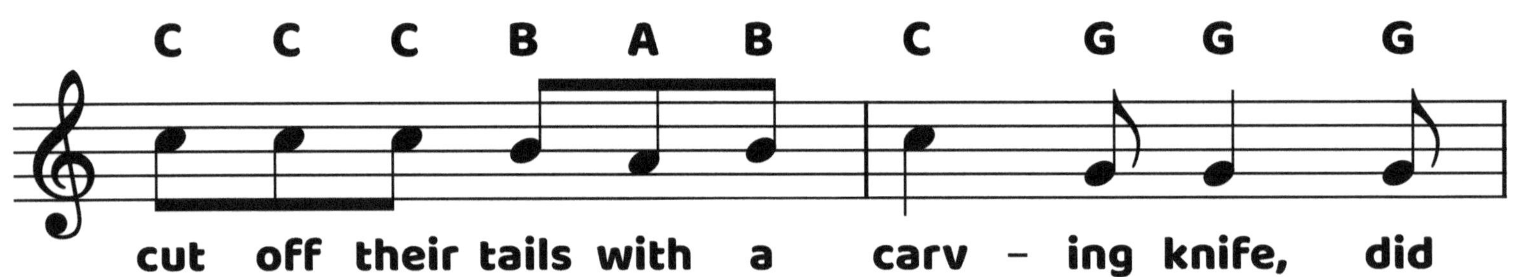

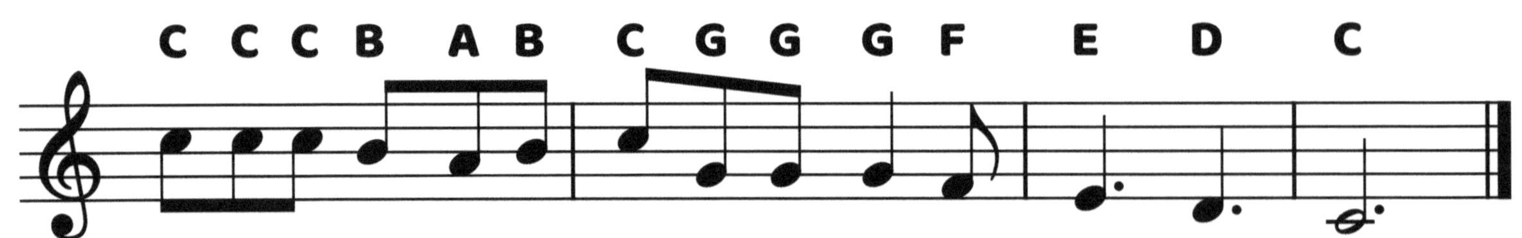

Twinkle Twinkle Little Star

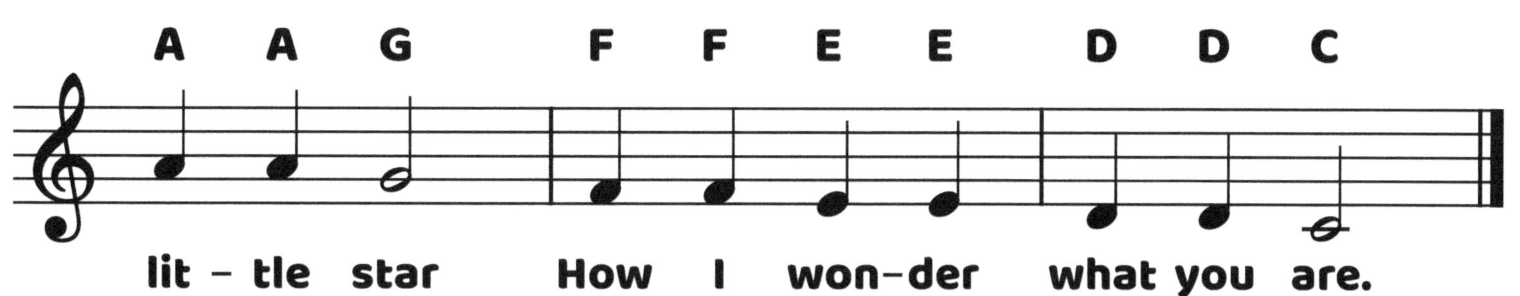

We Wish You a Merry Christmas

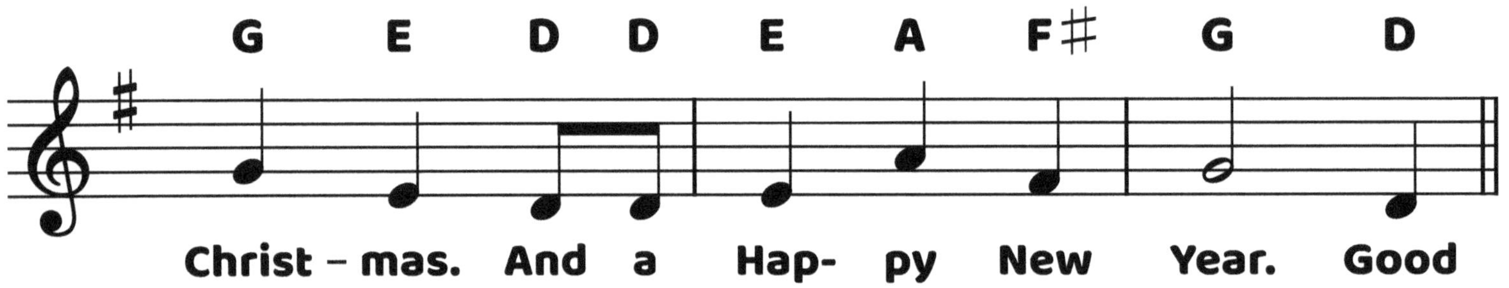

D   A   B   A G F♯ G   D   D   D   D
kin.   We   wish you a Mer-ry   Christ - mas.   And   a

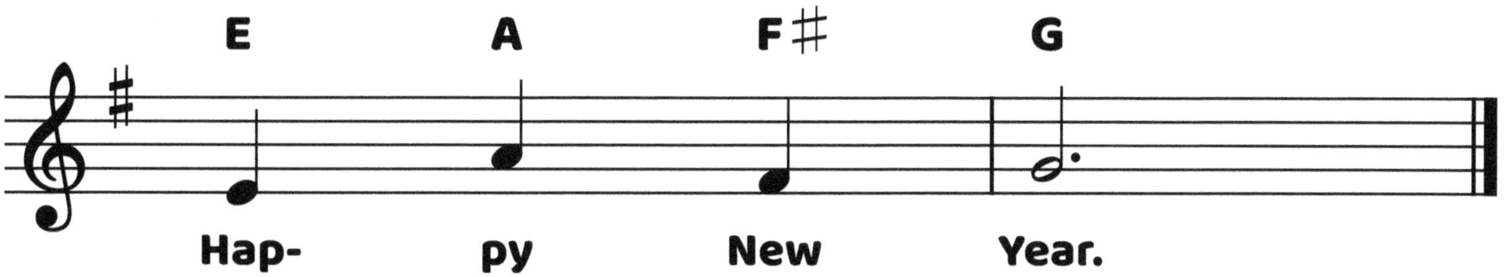

E   A   F♯   G
Hap-   py   New   Year.

White Christmas

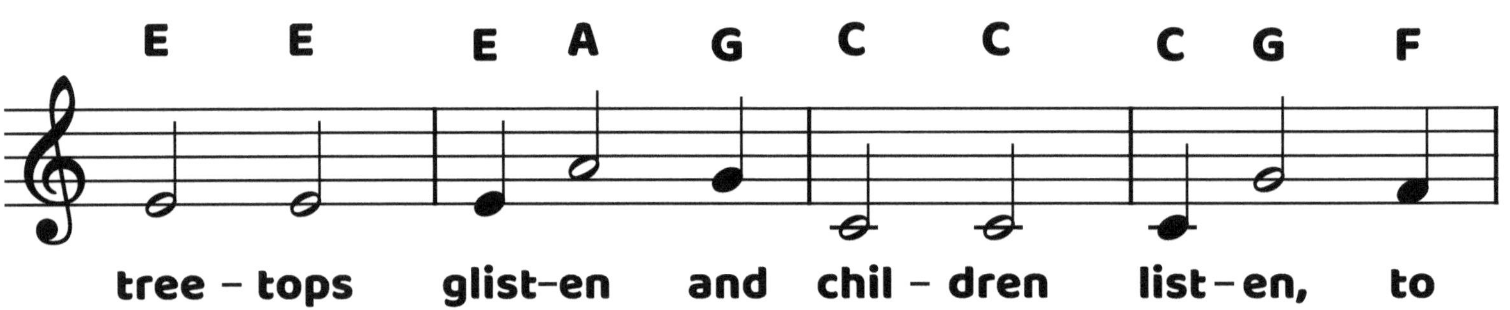

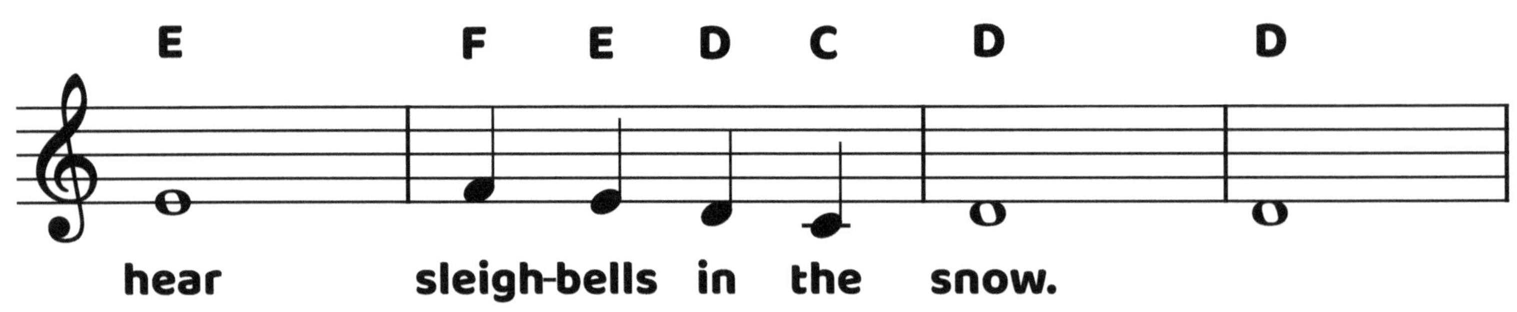

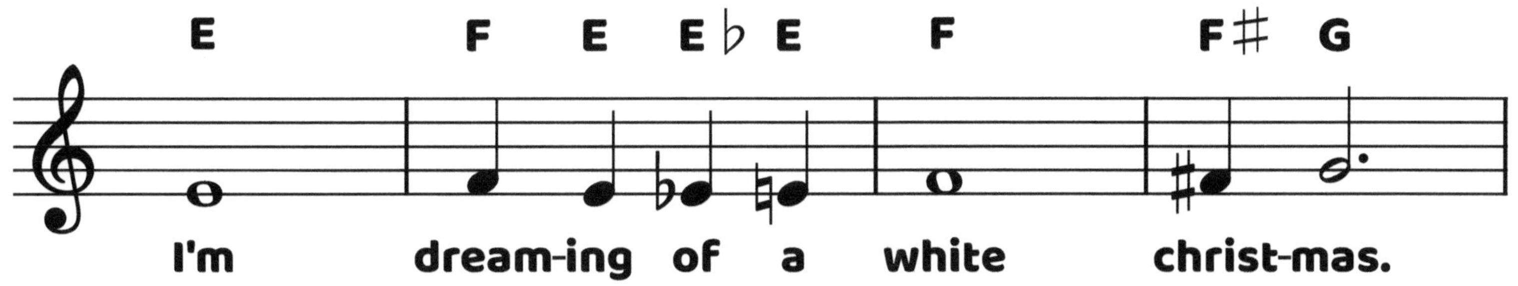

E   F E E♭ E   F   F♯ G
I'm   dream-ing of a   white   christ-mas.

A B C   D C B A   G   C D
With e–very   christ-mas card   I   write.   "May your

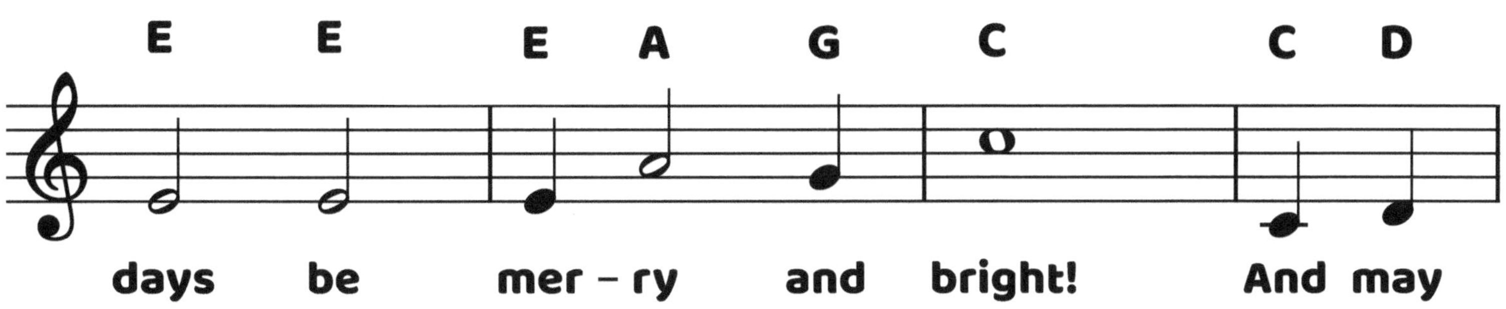

E   E   E A   G   C   C D
days   be   mer–ry   and   bright!   And may

E   E   A B B B   C
all   your   Christ–mas – es   be   white."

Danny Boy

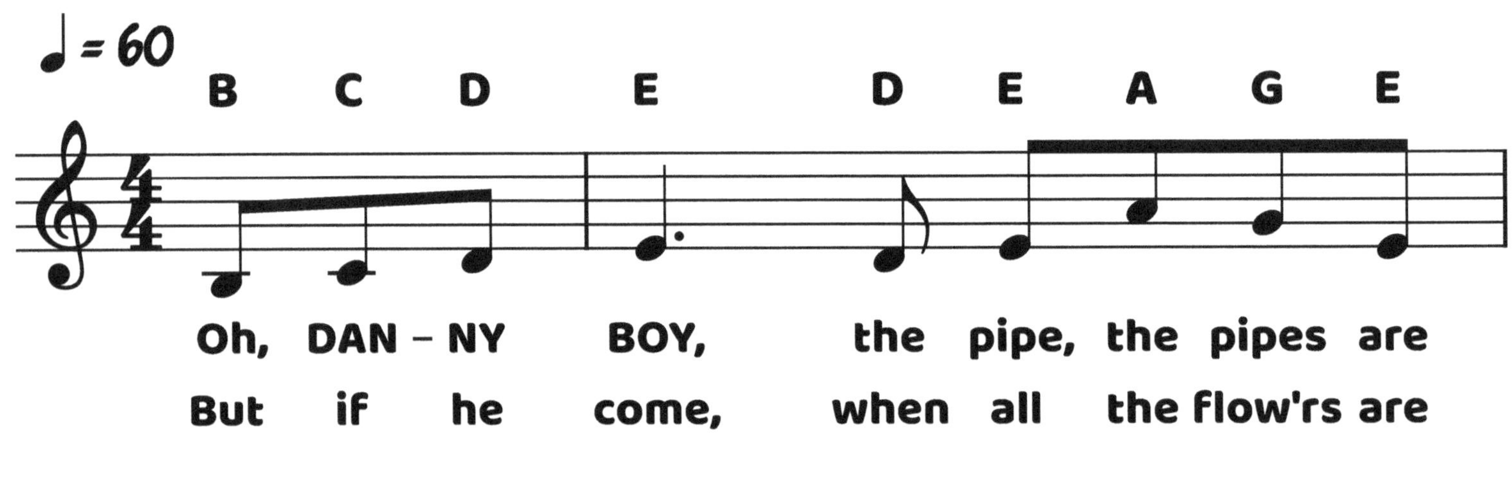

♩ = 60
B C D E D E A G E
Oh, DAN – NY BOY, the pipe, the pipes are
But if he come, when all the flow'rs are

D C A A C E F
call – ing,________ from glen to
dy – ing,________ and I am

G A G E C E D D B C D
glen, and down the moun–tain side.______ The sum–mer's
dead, as dead I well may be,______ ye'll come and

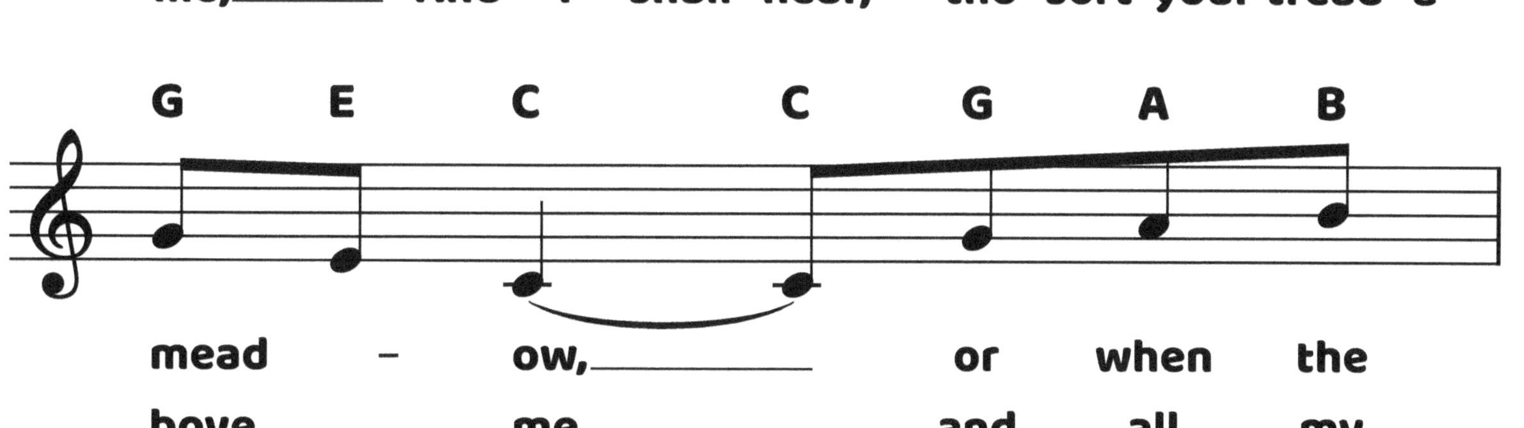

E D E A G E D C A A B C D

gone, and all the ros-es fall - ing,___ It's you, it's
find the place where I am ly - ing,___ andkneel and

E F E D C D

you must go and I must
say an A - ve there for

C C G A B C B B A G A

bide.___ But come ye back whensum-mer's in the
me;___ And I shall hear, tho' soft your tread a -

G E C C G A B

mead - ow,___________ or when the
bove___ me,___________ and all my

C B B A G E D D G G G
val - ley's hush'd and white with snow.____ 'Tis I'll be
dreams will warm and sweet-er be.____ If you will not

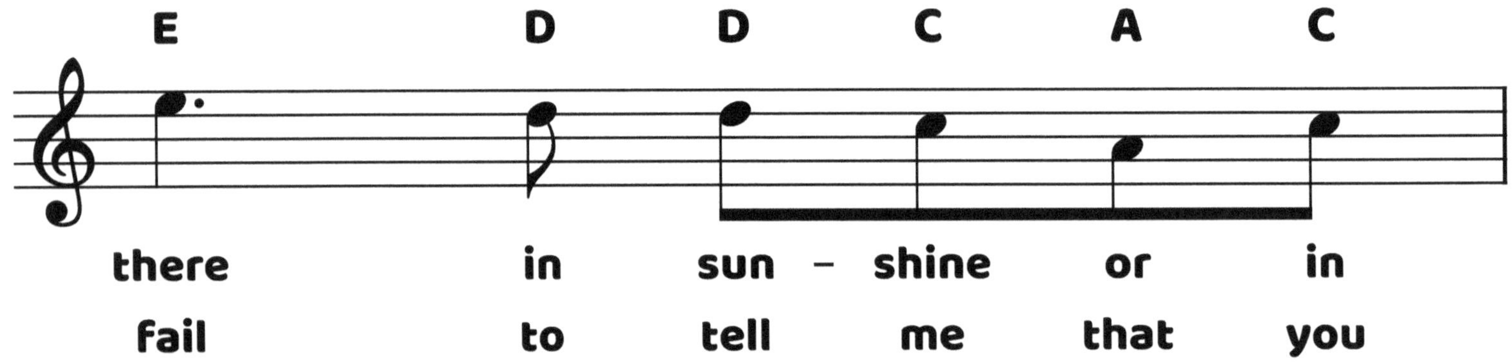

E D D C A C
there in sun - shine or in
fail to tell me that you

G E C C B C D E A G E D C A B
shad-dow, oh, DAN-NY BOY, oh DAN-NY BOY, I love you
love me,__then I shall sleep in peace un-til you come to

C
so!
me!

You Are My Sunshine

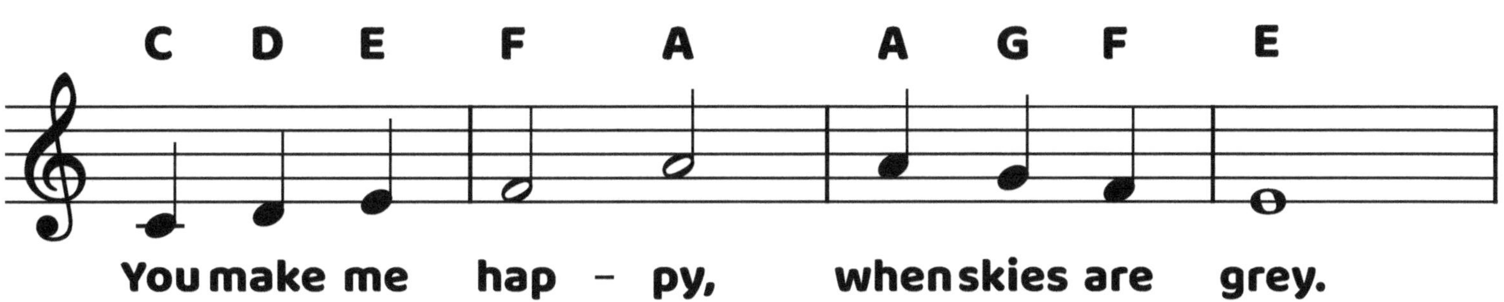

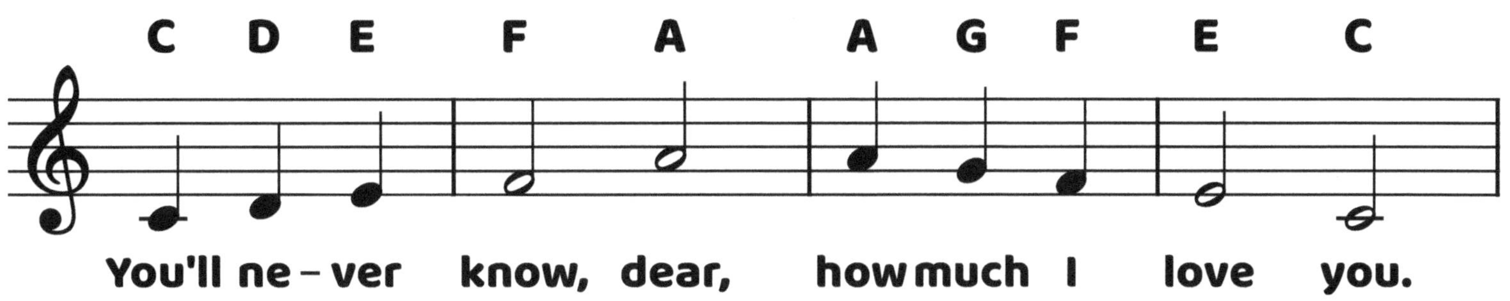

I've Been Working on the Railroad

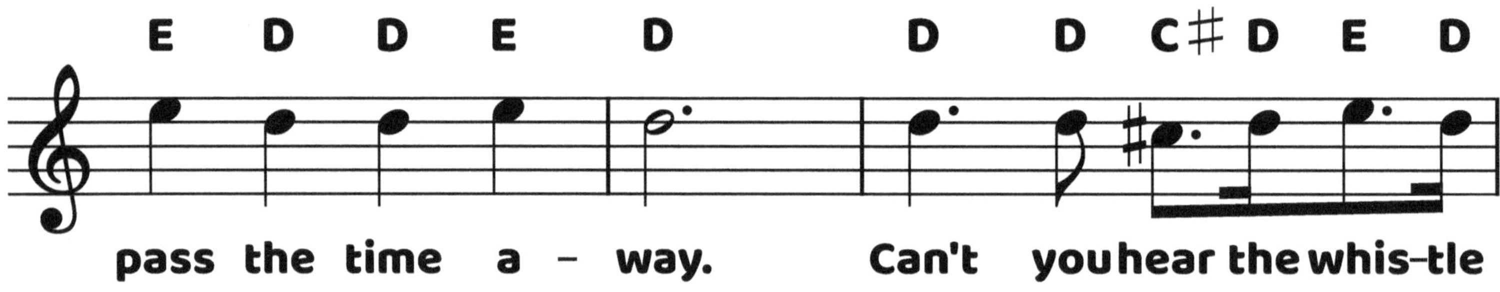

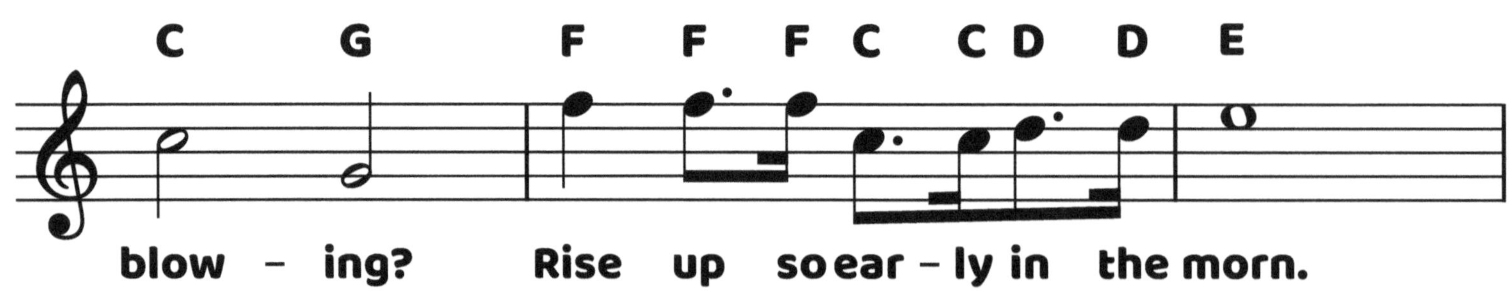

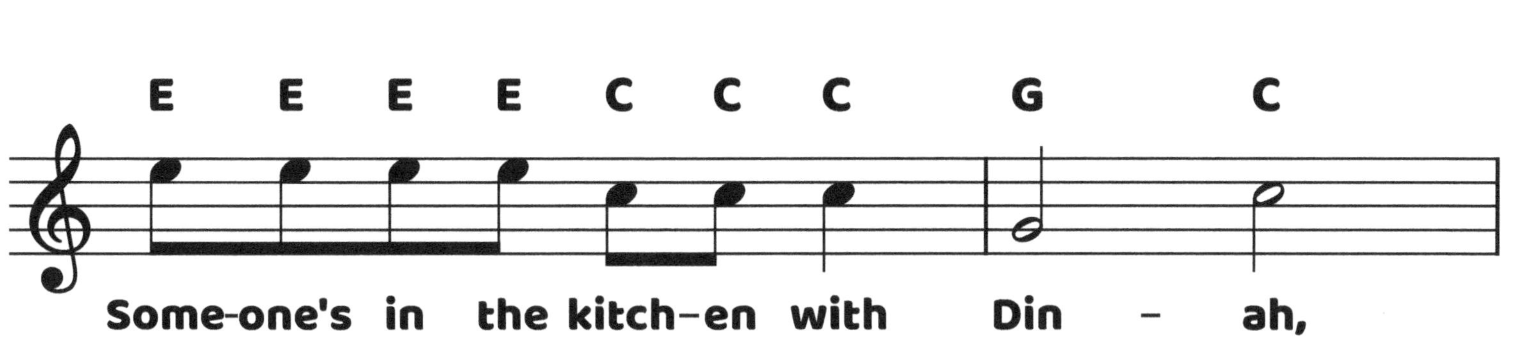

A B C B C A G C E F E D
Don't you hear the cap-tain shout – ing? "Din – ah, blow your
C G G G G C A A A A D
horn!" Din-ah won't you blow, Din-ah won't you blow,
B B B B A B C D E C
Din-ah won't you blow your horn?_______ horn?
E E E E C C C G C
Some-one's in the kitch-en with Din – ah,

E E E E C C C D B A G
Some-one's in the kit-chen I know,_______

E E E E C C C F A
Some-one's in the kit-chen with Din — ah

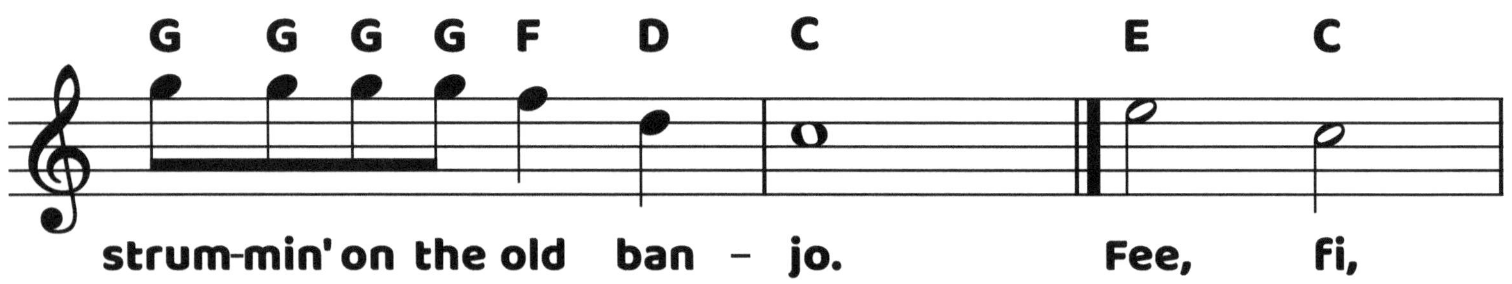

G G G G F D C E C
strum-min' on the old ban – jo. Fee, fi,

G G G C E E C C C C D B A G
3
fid-dle-ee-i – o, Fee, fi, fid-dle-ee-i – o,

E C F F F F A G G G G F D
3
Fee, fi, fid-dle-ee-i – o, strum-min' on the old ban–

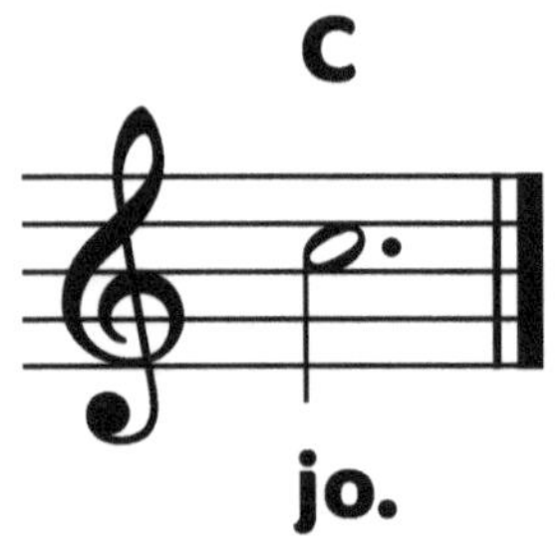

C
jo.

Old King Cole

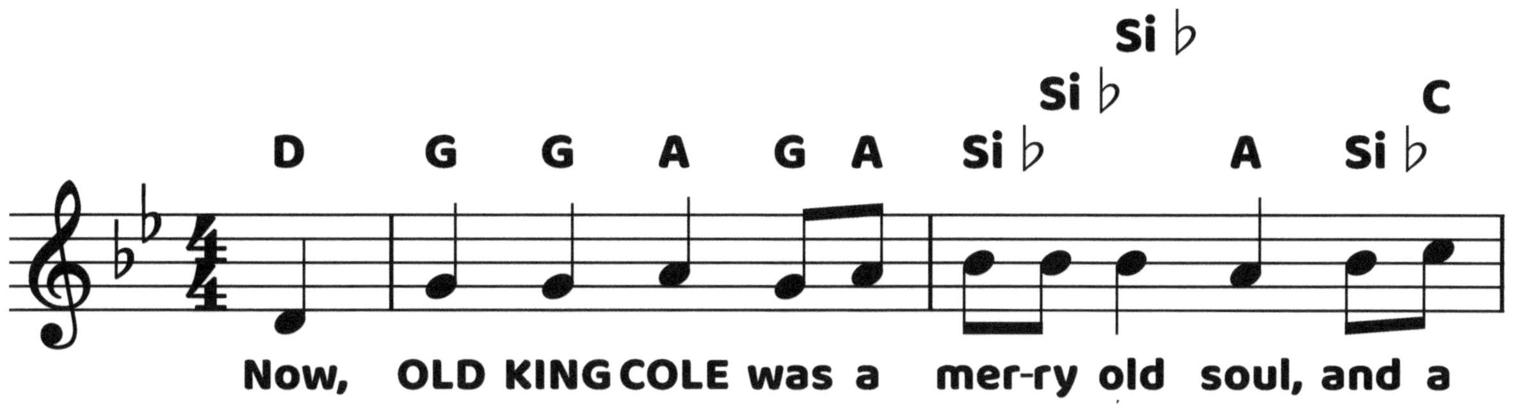

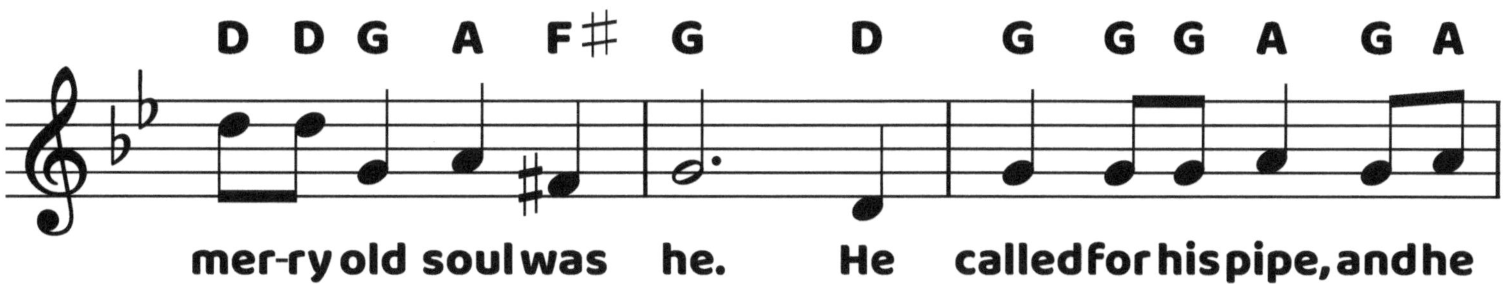

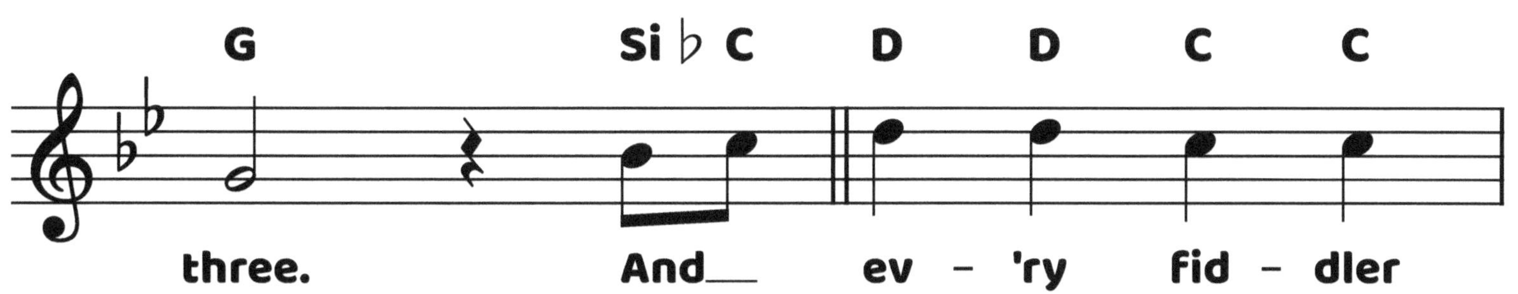

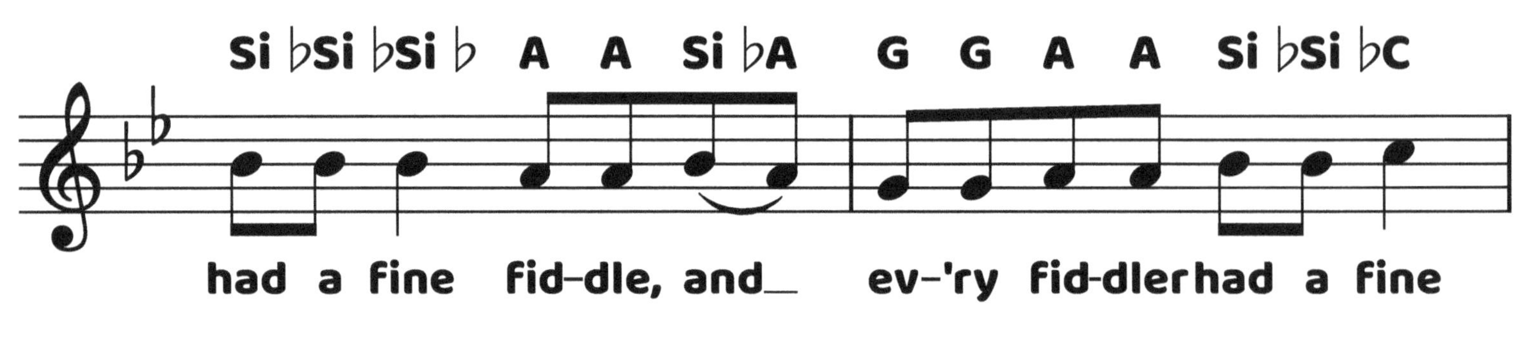

Si♭ Si♭ Si♭ A A Si♭ A G G A A Si♭ Si♭ C
had a fine fid-dle, and__ ev-'ry fid-dler had a fine

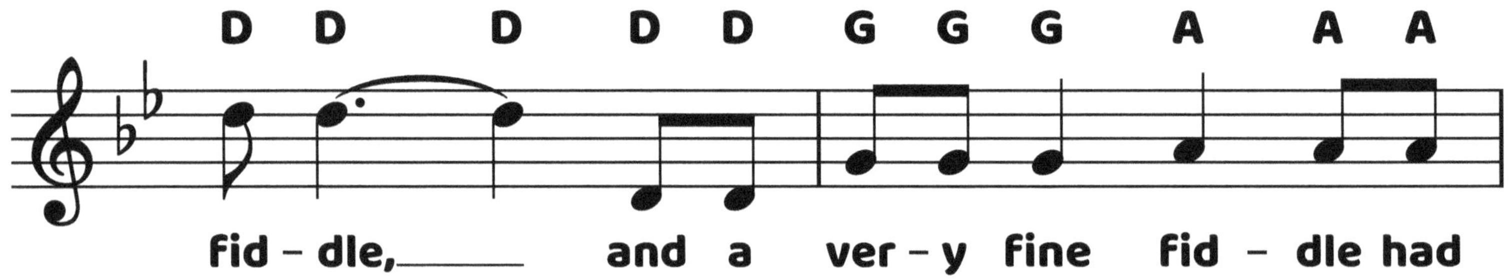

D D D D D D G G G A A A
fid - dle,______ and a ver - y fine fid - dle had

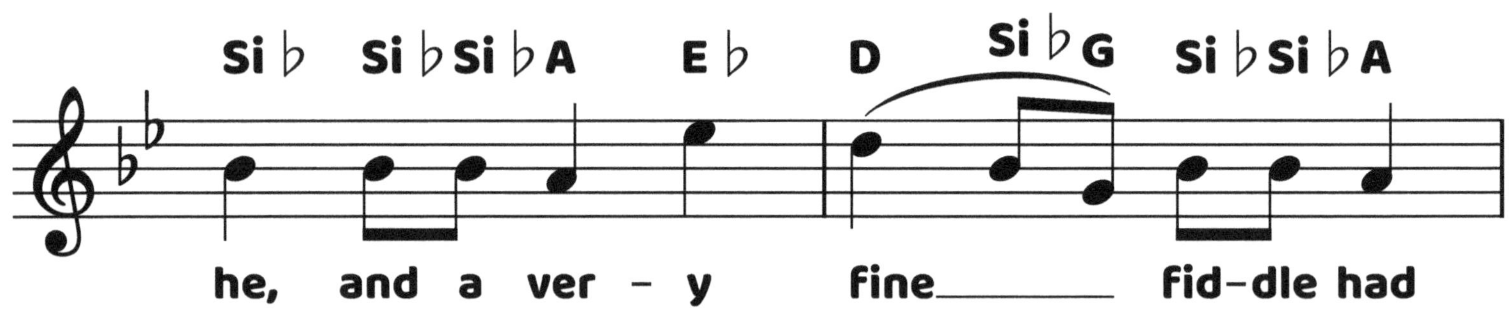

Si♭ Si♭ Si♭ A E♭ D Si♭ G Si♭ Si♭ A
he, and a ver - y fine______ fid-dle had

G Si♭ C D D C D C
he. For__ OLD KING COLE was a

Si♭ Si♭ Si♭ A Si♭ A G G A Si♭ C
mer-ry old sou, yes, a mer-ry old soul was

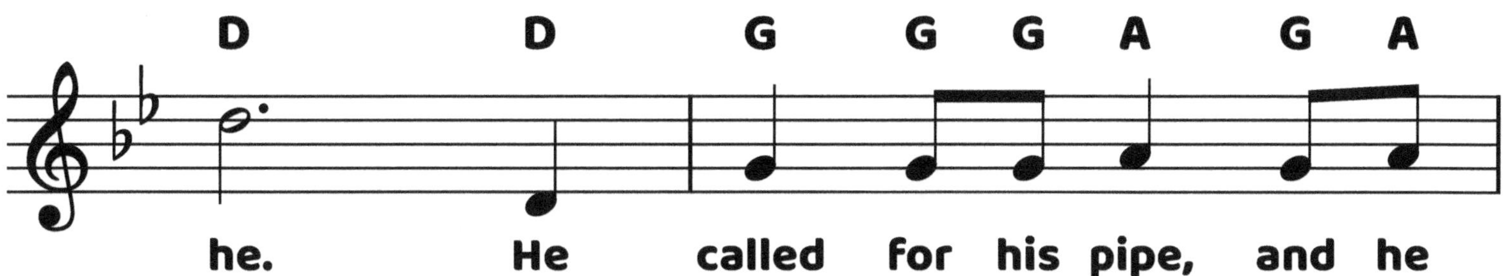

D   D   G   G G A   G A
he.   He   called for his pipe, and he

Si♭ Si♭ Si♭ A   Si♭ C   D   G G A   D
called for his bowl, and he   called for his fid – dlers

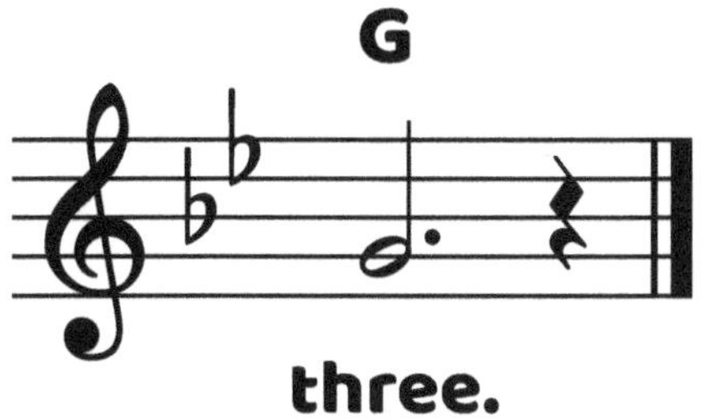

G
three.

Polly Wolly Doodle

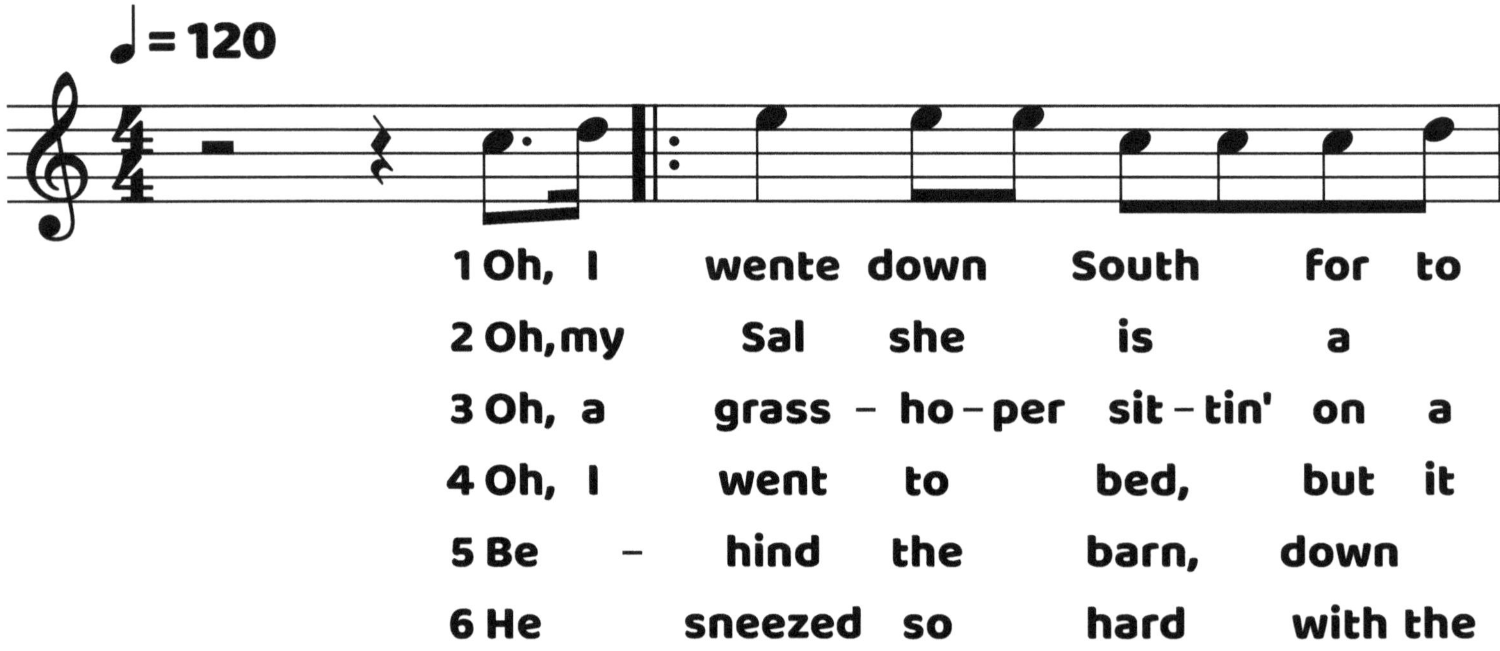

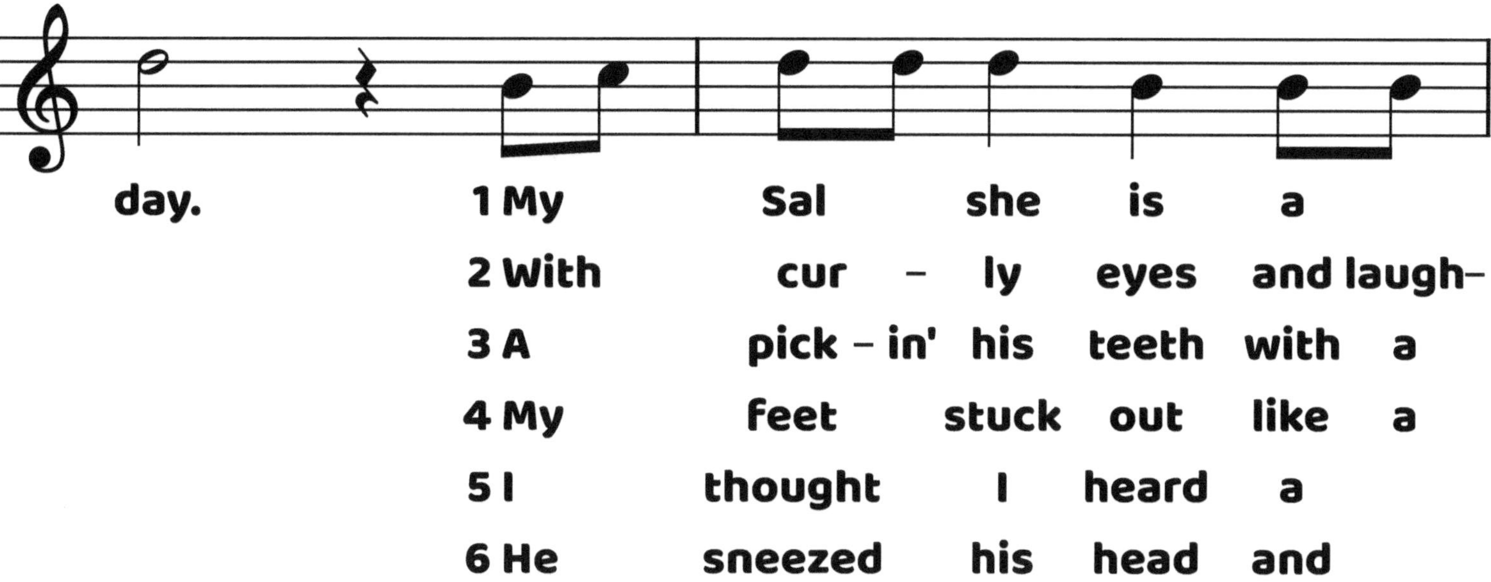

day.
1 My   Sal   she   is   a
2 With   cur – ly   eyes   and laugh–
3 A   pick – in' his   teeth   with a
4 My   feet   stuck   out   like   a
5 I   thought   I   heard   a
6 He   sneezed   his   head   and

spunk – y   gal, Sing-ing pol–ly wol–ly doo-dle all the
ing   hair,
car – pet   tack,
chick – en   roost,
chick – en   sneeze,
tail   right off,

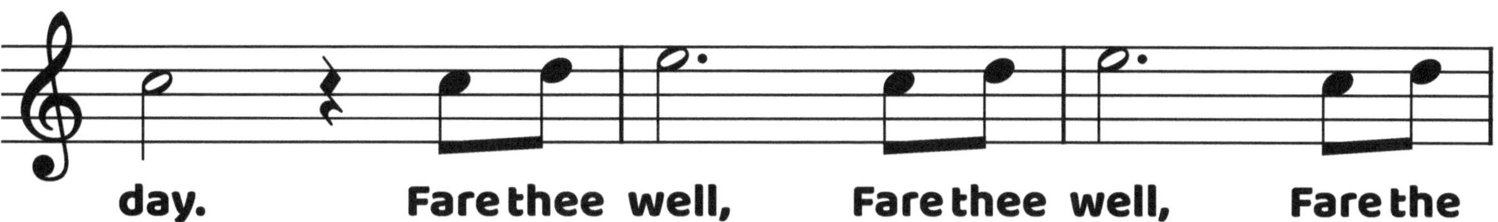

day.   Fare thee well,   Fare thee well,   Fare the

well, my fair - y fay, For I'm goin' to Lou'-si-an-a for to

see my Su - zi - an - na, Sing-ing pol-ly wol-ly doo-dle all the

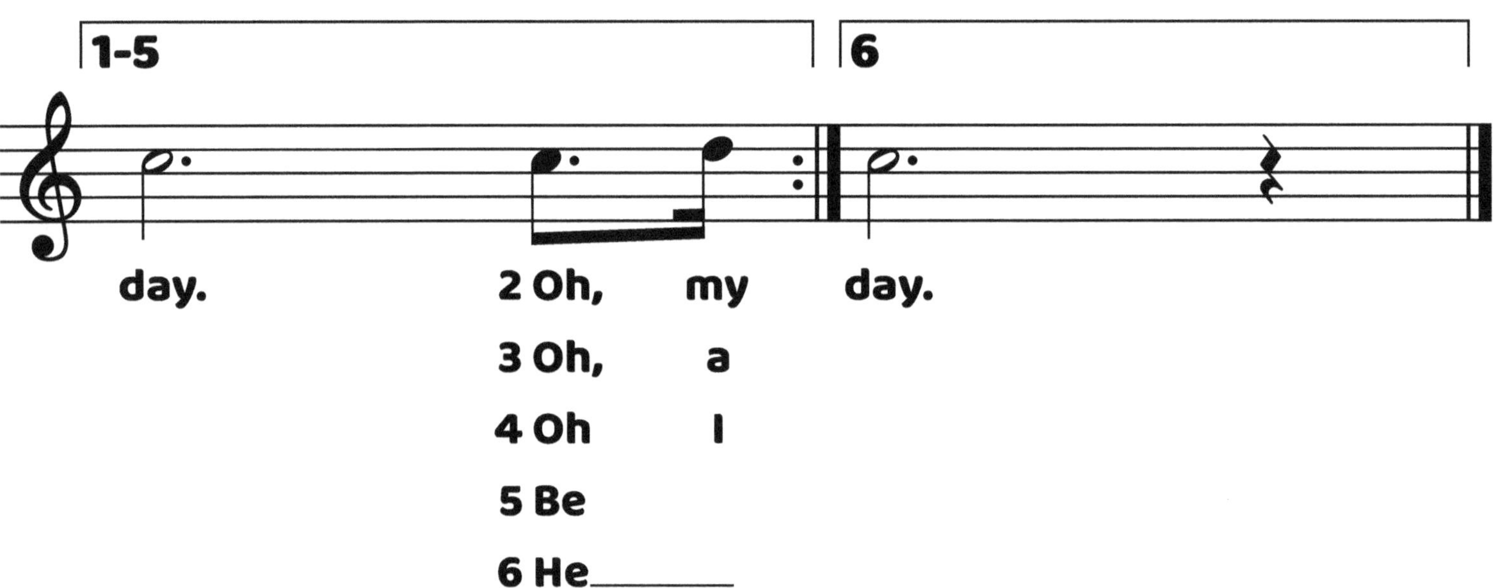

1-5
6
day.
2 Oh, my day.
3 Oh, a
4 Oh I
5 Be
6 He

GET YOUR FREE BONUS PIANO BOOK!

Your Opinion Matters! Help Us Shape the Future of Piano Music

Dear Valued Customer,

We hope this message finds you well and that your musical journey continues to be a harmonious and fulfilling one. We wanted to reach out to you today to express our heartfelt gratitude for choosing our piano book «EASY PIANO SHEET MUSIC SONGBOOK FOR KIDS PART 2», to be your companion on this melodious adventure.

As creators and musicians ourselves, we understand the pivotal role that feedback plays in refining and enhancing our craft. Your insights and opinions are invaluable to us, and we believe they have the power to shape the future of piano music. That's why we kindly request you to take a few moments out of your day to leave a review for «EASY PIANO SHEET MUSIC SONGBOOK FOR KIDS PART 2».

Your review will not only help us understand what aspects of the book resonated with you the most but also guide us in making improvements to provide an even more enriching experience for aspiring pianists like yourself. By sharing your thoughts, you become an integral part of our creative process, and your contribution will be felt by countless others who embark on this musical journey.

Whether you found the exercises particularly helpful, the sheet music beautifully arranged, or the accompanying explanations insightful, your honest review will help fellow musicians make informed decisions. Your words could be the encouragement someone else needs to dive into the world of piano music and unlock their artistic potential.

Leaving a review is easy:

*   Just click on the link and leave a good review if you like the book.

Thank you once again for choosing our book, and we eagerly await your insights. Together, we can create a harmonious and inspiring environment for every pianist to thrive.

May your music continue to resonate with passion and grace! Warm regards,

Henry White